CONTENTS

CHAPTER 1 CHAPTER

The world of oils

OIL PAINT has a richness, brilliance and intensity which are unmatched by any other medium. When oil first started to be used as a binder for pigment, some time in the fifteenth century, the new medium was admired for its jewel-like colours and smooth, almost glassy surface from which all evidence of the brush had been obliterated. Writers remarked upon the 'inner light' and luminosity of the new medium, which allowed light to be reflected back from the underpainting, through layers of transparent glazes. Later artists favoured a more expressive and personal approach, one in which the mark of the brush and evidence of the way the paint had been applied became important parts of the final image.

Artists today use a variety of approaches, building up thick, textured surfaces or thin veils of translucent colour, creating paint surfaces which are matt or glossy, thick or thin, textured or smooth, opaque or transparent. Oil provides the artist with an almost limitless range of possibilities, and once you have learnt to handle and enjoy this most rewarding of media, you will be limited only by your own ingenuity and imagination.

This intimate, domestic and very personal painting is by the artist Margaret Green. It is a view of a studio she once had, by the sea. The fireplace was a very intense blue, and the bright yellow chair was there in the studio when she took it over. The wonderful blue and yellow, together with the red of the flowers on the table, sing against the basic white and neutral tones of the room. The most ordinary subject becomes special when seen through the eyes of an artist.

THE PLEASURE OF PAINT

This book assumes no knowledge of painting or drawing, so if you are thinking, 'I can't draw', or, 'I haven't picked up a paint brush since I was eleven', this book is for you. However, it is also designed for those of you who have tried drawing or painting in another medium but haven't yet used oil.

What we do assume is that everyone is capable of handling paint and producing a visual image and, more importantly, that everyone can enjoy the experience. A lot of people think you need special talent to paint but this is no more true than thinking you need special ability to walk, to talk or to write. Everyone can paint and draw; after all, we all did so as children. Unfortunately, as we grow older, we lose our initial confidence and rely more and more on other people's assessments of our work – one thoughtless criticism from a teacher or parent and we vow never to paint again. We also tend to become over-concerned with the end product and lose our enjoyment of the 'process' of painting.

Painting should be a journey of exploration, discovery and pleasure. The artist sets off in a particular direction but ends up somewhere else, having learned a great deal and been entertained along the way. Great artists never lose that spirit of inquiry and are prepared to take risks and even to make mistakes. This is why their work is always fresh and stimulating – take Pablo Picasso (1881–1973), for example.

▷ *Richard Pikesley's paintings are characterized by lovely pearly colours, the soft light which suffuses them and the delicate but determined way in which he handles the paint. Richard says that his paintings are often 'triggered by light and the way it falls across forms and creates a sort of abstraction which is not necessarily the same as the forms themselves'. He says he likes 'that contradiction'. For many years he painted all his landscapes on site, but now he completes them in the studio. This allows him time to elaborate the painting. There is a risk in this approach because 'the thing that triggered you to do the painting in the first place might be something very simple which is best dealt with very simply. The great danger of studio painting is that it can become too fussy'.*

There are so many levels on which you can enjoy oil painting. There is something very special about the dazzling white of a newly primed canvas, the smell of paint and the springiness of a new brush. There is also the intellectual stimulation of composition, finding a subject that means something to you, looking for balance and harmony, and wrestling with the theoretical aspects of colour and perspective. And there is the pure sensual pleasure of paint, the way it moves on the canvas, streaking and dripping, building up into ridges and furrows or barely staining the surface.

In this book I try to convey that sense of enjoyment because I believe it is the best way to ensure that you will persevere until you produce paintings that give you pleasure and satisfaction.

△ The artist Jenny Rodwell is interested in small, intimate subjects – delicate china cups, a part of an interior or a bunch of wild flowers. She works on a small scale and uses a low-key palette. The paintings are not brightly coloured but they are nevertheless full of colour. The colours Jenny uses are slightly muted and relate to one another harmoniously. She 'draws' by making very precise observations of the changes of tone within the subject, so that the image emerges from the canvas. As her paintings are small, she works with thin paint and is not concerned with surface texture. She sometimes uses pencil to add darker tones, as in the background of this painting.

ABOUT THIS BOOK

Oil is a remarkably flexible and responsive medium. You can record your responses to a scene in a single sitting, or use a layered technique to develop a work in a series of considered stages over days, months or years. You can work into the wet paint, overpaint dry paint, scratch back into the paint surface, or even scrape it off and start again. You can work with brushes, knives, rags or even your fingers. Your work can be detailed, restrained and small-scale, or big, bold and expressive. You can paint figurative subjects or abstracts, flowers, people or animals, the view from your window or a collection of dishes – the choice is yours.

In this chapter, as throughout the book, I show the work of different artists to illustrate some of these approaches, subjects and concerns. This will give you a flavour of the limitless possibilities of oil paint and I trust that you'll find something to inspire you. For example, the three paintings of flowers on pages 7, 8 and 9 differ in almost every respect – shape, size, composition, the approach to colour and the way the paint is handled. All they share is the fact that they are paintings of flowers in oil on canvas.

I go on to look at materials and equipment and to review some of the products on the market. The rest of the book broadly divides into two sections. In the first I illustrate and describe simply and clearly the basic techniques, also defining the most helpful and frequently used terms. You'll get more from these sections if you have some paint to hand and start experimenting on cheap surfaces such as paper or card. It is important that you get used to the feel of the paint and the way it responds to the brush, the surface and different methods of handling. See how it feels when you use the paint straight from the tube; now try diluting it with a little turpentine; and next add a little linseed oil. You can read every book on painting techniques, but there is no substitute for the 'hands-on' experience – and anyway, it's more fun.

In the final section of the book I illustrate three step-by-step projects which incorporate the techniques and approaches discussed elsewhere. These projects allow you to 'look over the artist's shoulder', to see a work in progress and to learn from that experience. Although you might want to copy some of these projects, you'll learn much more by setting up or finding an equivalent subject of your own but then approaching it in the same way as the artist.

I recommend that you start by working broadly, using a larger brush than you might normally choose. Many people are inhibited when they start to paint, but by adopting a bold, rather 'attacking' approach you can overcome any beginner's block and start to learn about painting. As you become more confident and skilled, you will evolve your own approach. You may decide that big brushes and swirling colour are for you, or you may feel that a restrained approach on a smaller scale is better suited to your personality and intentions.

▽ *The artist Margaret Thomas describes* Bluebells and Donkey *as 'an attempt to harness the casual, while at the same time exploiting the inherent characteristics of familiar and loved objects, strictly in terms of oil paint.'*

△ Here is a dramatic approach to the subject of flowers. The artist, Ian Sidaway, has worked on a large scale and has chosen to make a study of full-blown tulips, just before the petals start to drop. The main elements of the painting are placed within the bottom half of the work, so that the large area of neutral grey becomes an important part of the composition. The pattern of shadows provides yet another theme. The paint surface is flat and matt, the edges of the images crisp and clean. By carefully orchestrating the separate elements, the artist has made a beautiful image from an apparently simple subject.

EXPLORING A SUBJECT

In this series of four small paintings all made on the same day, the artist, Ian Sidaway, was exploring an idea which he hoped to work up into a larger painting. He often uses photographs for reference, taking photos especially for this purpose, though his paintings are never direct copies. In this case he first made a number of drawings and watercolour sketches, taking images from a variety of sources. Some of the figures were photographed in the sea in France, others in a pool in the United States.

As you can see, he is moving the figure around, seeing what happens, sometimes apparently breaking compositional rules by placing it off to one side. However, he uses various devices to create a harmonious image, balancing the swimmer by areas of darker tone, reflections or the pattern of ripples. The water is treated in a variety of ways – in one case, an abstract tracery of lines; in others, more realistically and loosely rendered. He abandoned the idea of working the painting up on a larger scale; he had done all he wanted with the subject and felt it would not work so well as a larger piece.

△ In this study the pattern-making qualities of the waves are explored.

◁ Here the swimmer is placed almost dead centre, with darker areas balancing the picture. The paint surface is energetically handled.

▷ Because the artist describes the surroundings in greater detail, this picture has a less abstract quality.

△ *This study has a more three-dimensional quality because the edge of the pool is included.*

DRAWING AND SKETCHING

To be a good artist you must learn to look and really 'see' the world around you. 'Of course I can see', you may say, but can you? We often think we 'know' what things look like, but as soon as you pick up a pencil and start to draw, you'll find that peculiar things happen – a table you thought was square suddenly isn't, an object you know to be round looks flat, and a seated figure looks, well, impossible. To interpret the visual world in paint, you must first learn to 'see' it, and one of the very best ways of doing this is to draw . . . constantly.

All artists draw constantly. They draw to increase their understanding of what they see, to record a passing idea and as a record of their daily life. For many artists their sketch books are their most valuable possession, the source of all their art.

So let's start. Look around and focus on some familiar object in the room – a chair, for example. Now really look at it and get to know it. Remove from your mind all preconceived ideas of what a chair is and see it as an abstract object. First, see it as a pattern of lights and darks. Half close your eyes to emphasize the tonal constrasts. If you have a pen or pencil to hand, put down the dark areas with quick, scribbly lines – don't worry how it looks, just get it down. When you've finished, look at it and you'll find that those apparently abstract blobs of light and dark do describe a chair.

Now, half closing your eyes again, draw the spaces around the chair, the space between the chair and a nearby table, for example. Continue in this way, working quickly, and again you'll find that you've recorded another aspect of the object we call a chair.

Next, study the quality of the edges. Notice the way a plane in shadow has a sharp edge when seen against a light area and a soft edge when seen against a dark area. Now look at the colours. A good way of making yourself really see them is to allow your eyes to travel over the surface of the chair and describe the colours to yourself. For instance, at this moment I'm looking at a typist's swivel chair seen against the light. I know the seat is covered in a medium-charcoal, tweedy fabric, but the back of the chair seen against the light appears a deep, matt blue-black, while the area where the light falls across the seat is quite pale by contrast – a bluey grey. The top surfaces of the chrome base are very pale indeed – a silvery colour with touches of yellow, pink and blue picked up from the surroundings – while the areas in shadow are dark – not as dark as the chair back but considerably darker than the chair seat.

Make sure you always have a pencil and paper near you and get into the habit of drawing every day. Draw ordinary things, like the cups and plates on the breakfast table, the plant at the window, a friend watching television. Take a small sketchbook with you when you go out so that you can jot down things that interest you. Learn to draw quickly and from memory . . . and don't worry what the drawings look like. No one else need see them and years later you'll be surprised and pleased to find that a very brief sketch can stir memories of an image or an event as well as providing you with a valuable source of visual material and ideas.

Stan Smith is fascinated by the play of light on the figure and the way it reveals and conceals forms, creating abstraction in a figurative work. Here are pages from his sketchbooks which deal with this theme. These drawings were made over a period of time using whatever medium was convenient and close to hand. Stan draws constantly and has done so all his life. In his sketchbooks he makes notes of things that catch his eye, jots down ideas and develops themes. On the next page is a painting based on the themes in these sketches.

MAKING PICTURES

Many amateur artists are wholly concerned with 'copying' from nature and judge their success or failure as artists by the accuracy with which they can replicate what they see. It is important to work from life, developing your powers of perception and your skill with paint so that you can describe the world competently and accurately. As with language, when you move on from studying grammar and vocabulary to creative composition, so in painting you can move on from exercises that merely improve your visual and manual dexterity to more ambitious and exciting projects. In this book I explore the idea of 'making pictures', how the artist edits, organizes and orchestrates the elements in the world to make an image which is entirely unique.

On this page I show a painting by Stan Smith. He has made many studies of the play of light on the figure, and on the previous pages we saw some sketchbook drawings in which he dealt with just this theme. He worked on this particular painting for over a year and in that time it changed radically. Initially, the figure sat along the bottom of the painting, with the huge window occupying the space above, but he wasn't satisfied with the way the composition was working. He left it for a while, thought about it and finally reworked it, lifting the figure up the picture area to let the light shine through underneath. This changed the geometry and emphasis, creating a strong image which sticks in the mind.

▽ This sketch is in oil, pencil and oil pastel on paper. It is sometimes assumed that oil is only appropriate for finished paintings on canvas or board, but it can also be used for quick sketches on other supports. The paper can be prepared with a coat of size or primer, which will seal it and prevent the oil from bleeding into the paper, causing the pigment to become dry and flake off. For quick sketches which you don't intend to keep you can paint straight on to the paper.

▷ This is a large painting in which the artist explores a favourite theme. He worked on it intermittently for over a year, changing the composition radically at one stage.

△ *In this detail you can see the way the paint has been used – thinly in some areas, so that it barely stains the canvas, while other areas are heavily overlaid. The way the artist has invented colour is particularly interesting. Look, for example, at the flesh tones, where you can see every colour but pink, including ochres, light red and a very dark viridian green. If you look closely, you can see that he has also mixed his media, using dashes of oil pastel in the shadows cast by the blind.*

CHAPTER 2 CHAPTER

Supports

THE WORD SUPPORT describes any surface which carries or 'supports' the paint. Canvas is the most popular support for oil paint; in fact, the word is often used as a synonym for oil painting. There is something very special about the way that canvas responds to the brush, and nothing else matches its liveliness and spontaneity. Unfortunately, canvas, especially ready-stretched and primed, is impossibly expensive if you paint frequently, so it is important to get to know the wide range of cheaper supports that are available, and to find out which you like.

An artist is also a craftsman, so you will need to become familiar with your materials and learn how to prepare, handle and, above all, enjoy them. It is said that 'a poor craftsman blames his tools', implying that a superior one can produce good work no matter what materials he has to work with. This may be true, but a good craftsman will produce even better work given the best materials, and as for the rest of us, we need all the help we can get! So, don't make false economies; buy the best materials and equipment you can afford, then spend time preparing them properly and looking after them. In this way they will last longer, give better results and be more fun to use.

△*All sorts of materials can be used as supports for oil painting. From left to right: muslin, scrim, cardboard, hardboard (rough and smooth sides), canvas, two kinds of oil sketching paper and cartridge paper.*

◁ *Preparing your own supports is immensely satisfying. It also gives you a great deal of flexibility – you can control the size, the shape and the type of surface and save yourself a great deal of money as well. Here tacks are tapped through canvas, into a stretcher.*

▽ *From left: stretched canvas, hardboard, unprimed canvas, cartridge paper, primed cotton duck, primed linen canvas, oil sketching paper, stretchers and wedges.*

CHOOSING A SUPPORT

An important requirement of any support for oil painting is that it should not absorb the oil from the paint. If the oil is leached out, the paint surface will become dry, the pigment will lose its bond and eventually the paint will crack and flake off. Another problem is that oil rots many materials. A good oil support must also have sufficient 'tooth' or texture to hold the paint. On a smooth, polished surface the paint will slip and slide and will be difficult to work.

The type of surface you choose will depend on personal taste and the way you work. If your technique is closely worked and detailed and you use thin paint and fine brushes, you will probably feel happier with a fine-grained canvas or even a gesso ground (see page 27). If, however, you work in a bolder, broader way with thick swathes of paint on a large surface, you may prefer a more textured support – a coarse-grained canvas, for example. You might even use different supports for different purposes. In time and by trial and error you'll find a particular range that suits you.

Canvas

Stretched and primed canvas is a marvellously sympathetic surface on which to paint. The flexibility of the cloth responds to the pressure of the brushstroke, while the weave gives the surface a 'bite' which holds the paint and contributes a pleasing texture to the final paint surface. Another advantage of canvas is its portability – it is light, can be stored rolled before use, and when the painting is dry it can be removed from the stretcher, rolled up again and put away. Canvas can be bought in lengths off the roll or you can invest in a whole roll and cut it to size. There is a choice of fabrics, weights, widths and weaves to suit every taste, pocket and purpose.

Linen is probably the best and certainly the most expensive. It is made from the retted (rotted) stalks of flax and retains the dark brownish-grey colour of unbleached linen. Linen canvases are incredibly strong and hard-wearing, and are ideal for larger works where dimensional stability is particularly important.

Cotton is the other material used for artists' canvases and is generally cheaper. Cotton duck is a stout, densely woven cotton with an even weave. It provides a good, reasonably priced support suitable for most purposes. The main disadvantage of cotton is its tendency to stretch or shrink depending on the amount of moisture in the air. This becomes more pronounced and more of a problem the larger the canvas is. Wedges driven into the back of the stretcher will tauten the canvas again.

Both linen and cotton are available in different weights, weaves and qualities, from very fine to quite coarse and slubby. The majority of artists' suppliers have a choice of the most popular types of canvas. Select a width that will produce the least waste when you cut it. Study the advertisements from canvas suppliers in specialist art magazines, and if there is one near you, visit it; there is no substitute for actually handling the material when choosing a support. If you are lucky, they'll have some cheap offcuts with which you can experiment. Otherwise there are many suppliers that dispatch materials by mail-order nationwide.

Canvas can also be bought on the roll ready-primed. Some will be primed with an acrylic primer suitable for both oil and acrylic paints; some is sized and primed with an oil primer for use with oil paint only.

Other materials that can be used as supports include linen and cotton mixtures, and hessian.

Stretched canvases

Ready-stretched and primed canvases are available in a range of standard sizes. They are primed with either an acrylic ground or an oil-based primer. Check the texture. Some are fine-grained and suitable for detailed work; others are coarser.

Wood supports

The earliest oil paintings were painted on wooden panels, but these were soon superseded by canvas. Wood panels are heavy, expensive and difficult to prepare. If you do have access to wood panels, make sure they are well seasoned to minimize warping. Battening the back and sizing both sides will also help to stabilize them.

Canvas boards

The great advantage of canvas boards is that they require no preparation as they are supplied primed with an oil or acrylic ground. They have a good tooth, and are available with very fine or slightly more textured surfaces, and in a good range of sizes. They are ideal for the beginner who doesn't want to spend too much money and has neither the time nor the facilities to prepare any of the other cheap supports I have described.

Oil sketching papers

The cheapest and simplest of all the ready-mades are the oil sketching papers. These are inexpensive embossed papers primed for use with oil paints or oil pastels. They have a range of surfaces from very fine to coarse, with a variety of embossed patterns which loosely replicate the texture of canvas. Light and available as large sheets or sketching pads, they are useful for making notes and experimenting. The pads are particularly convenient as they provide a firm surface for when you are out sketching.

STRETCHING CANVAS

To stretch an unprimed canvas you'll need canvas, scissors, tacks, four stretcher pieces, wooden wedges or keys and a hammer. Stretchers vary in length, width and the way they are bevelled. The weight of the stretcher depends on the size of canvas you are stretching; the larger the canvas the heavier the stretcher, and for really large canvases you'll need a crossbar, possibly two. Canvas puts the wooden stretcher pieces under some strain and a large stretcher may come apart if you don't use a crossbar.

Fit the four stretcher pieces together, making sure that the bevelled edges are on the underside – these bevels prevent the stretcher from cutting into the canvas. The stretchers we used here were bevelled on both sides. Tap the corners gently with a mallet for a firm fit. Lay the frame on the canvas, making sure that the edges are parallel to the weave. You must get the canvas square; if you cut it on the cross, it will stretch unevenly and in time will become floppy. Cut the canvas with scissors or a craft knife and a metal straight-edge or steel rule, allowing a 2-in (5-cm) overlap on all four sides and making sure all the time that you are cutting parallel to the weave.

Fold the fabric over one stretcher and tack it or staple in the centre. Now do the same on the opposite side. If you are working on a large canvas, you may need canvas pliers to give you enough leverage to get the canvas really taut. Now tack the other two sides in the centre, making sure the canvas is taut without being overstretched – it should be springy to the touch but not tight as a drum. Test the surface of the ready-stretched canvases in your art suppliers to get a feel for the tension you are after. If the canvas is too tight, you can always take it off the stretchers and start again.

Continue tacking the canvas, working from the centre of the stretcher to the corners finishing with a flat, neat fold as illustrated. You shouldn't need wedges with small canvases, or even with large linen canvases, because linen is fairly stable, but if a canvas does begin to flop, you can put in wedges to tauten it again. Start on opposite corners and work round the canvas until it is properly stretched. Don't ram one set of wedges home or you'll exert more pressure in one direction than another. The trick is to keep the canvas square and evenly stretched in every direction. With practice you'll get a feel for what is just right.

△ *You will need canvas, four stretcher pieces, scissors or a craft knife and a straight edge, eight wooden keys and a hammer. A staple gun is a quick way of fixing the canvas to the stretcher. If the canvas is large, you may also need a pair of canvas pliers.*

△ *Slot the stretcher pieces together, making sure they are absolutely square at the corners. You don't need to bother with a set square; just check the stretcher corners against the corner of a table, or measure the diagonals with a tape measure to make sure they are identical.*

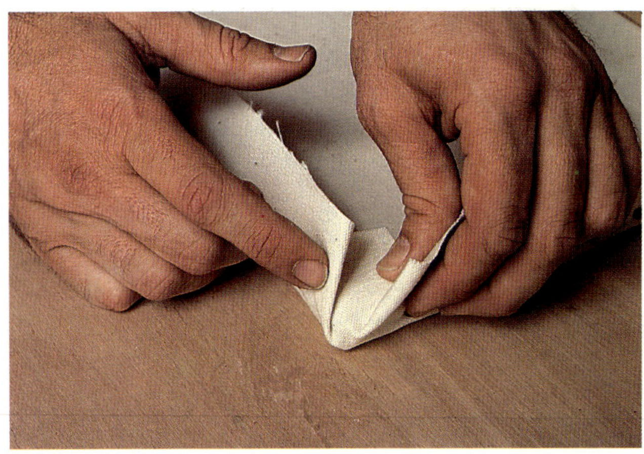

△ *Fold in the flap of canvas at the corner as shown, making the fold as flat and neat as possible. Tack it.*

△ *Lay the canvas face down and place the assembled stretcher, bevel edge down, on top of it. The bevel prevents the canvas being marked by the length of the stretcher behind it. Cut the canvas to size, allowing a 2-in (5-cm) overlap all round.*

▽ *Fix the canvas with one tack inserted in the centre of one side of the frame, pull it tightly across to the other side and tack it there. Repeat this on the other two sides. Now insert tacks on either side of the central tacks, working on one side then the opposite side and so on. Repeat this, working out from the centre towards the corners.*

△ *If there is any slack in the canvas, it can be taken up by tapping keys into the corners, but don't overdo it. With a canvas as small as this one, it shouldn't be necessary.*

SIZING AND PRIMING CANVAS

Canvas is highly absorbent and must be sealed to prevent the paint seeping into the fabric. This protects the canvas from the oil and the chemicals in the pigments, and also makes the surface easier to work. Painting on raw canvas is hard work, because the canvas absorbs the oil so quickly that paint becomes difficult to apply or move around the surface. Other absorbent supports, like paper, cardboard and hardboard, also need to be sealed.

The surface applied to a support is called the ground. There are many different grounds, and you'll have to experiment to find the one that suits you. A traditional ground consists of a couple of coats of glue size, which seals the surface, then a coat of white oil primer. Acrylic primers are applied directly to the support.

Making Size

The conventional way of sealing canvas is with glue size. The best and most flexible is rabbit-skin glue, which you will find in powder, crystal, solid or ready-made liquid forms. Most suppliers include directions for the preparation of size, but generally the size is left to soak in cold water, causing it to swell. It is then heated to dissolve the crystals and applied to the canvas with a brush while still warm.

Size is an ideal growing medium for mould, so if there is any left, cover and store it in a cool place. If mould does grow, simply scrape it off. To use the size again, reheat it. If you don't have an old saucepan, use a jam jar. Reheat by standing it in hot water.

△ **Preparing size** *Rabbit-skin glue is available in several forms including crystals or solid squares. You will need a container in which to heat the glue size.*

▽ *As a rough rule of thumb, use one cup of glue crystals to seven cups of water. Put the crystals in an old saucepan or glue pot, add the water and leave the crystals to swell and absorb all the water. At this stage they will look fluffy.*

◁ *Warm the mixture over a low heat. To avoid heating over a naked flame, put the size in a pot or jar which can in turn be placed in a saucepan of warm water. Stir with a wooden spoon or stick and the crystals will dissolve, producing a clear, viscous solution.*

▽ *Apply the warm size to the right side of the canvas with a large brush. Work from side to side with broad, sweeping strokes. As the size cools, it will become gelatinous.*

△ **Priming canvas** *An excellent ground suitable for canvas, hardboard or card can be prepared by mixing an acrylic emulsion glaze with equal parts of a water-based household emulsion paint. Apply two coats to the stretched canvas.*

Priming Canvas

You can paint directly on to the sized surface, but most artists prefer to apply a white ground or primer first. This creates yet another layer between the support and the paint, and provides a pleasant and responsive surface on which to work. Also the whiteness of the ground gives the painting an added brilliance and sparkle, and will counteract any tendency for paint to darken with age.

Oil primers are particularly flexible, but they take a long time to dry and should not be used for paintings in acrylic – remember this if you are likely to do an acrylic underpainting. You can buy oil primers ready-made from artists' suppliers or a good-quality oil-based undercoat will do equally well. Apply at least two coats, allowing the primer to dry completely between coats. Apply primer liberally so the pores of the canvas are filled; otherwise you will need a great deal of paint to cover the canvas.

Acrylic primers provide a modern, one-step ground which is applied directly to the support. I have used an acrylic emulsion glaze mixed with emulsion paint.

CHEAP SUPPORTS

Canvas is the support which automatically springs to mind when we think of oil painting, but there are a great many other surfaces which can be used. Some are cheap, others are easy to prepare, and others still are suited to particular styles of painting and particular purposes.

If you are not careful, it is possible to spend a great deal of money on materials and equipment. However, if you are to improve your skills and devclop your ideas, it is essential that you always have painting materials to hand. Here we look at ways of producing good, cheap supports and ways of recycling waste paper and card.

△ **Sizing paper** *Brush warm size on to paper and leave it to dry. If the paper is thin, it may crinkle. To prevent this, you should stretch it on a board. Take the sized paper, place it on a wooden board and tape all four sides with gummed paper. Leave to dry. Cut it from the board when it is dry. It will be perfectly flat. Paper can also be primed with acrylic primer. Apply a coat of primer with a brush and leave to dry. You can apply another coat when the first is dry.*

△ **Preparing cardboard** *Any cardboard can be used as a support, but the thick board used for cartons and packing is particularly good as it is firm and sturdy. Cut the cardboard using a craft knife and a straight edge.*

△ *Apply acrylic primer, working briskly with a large brush. Because cardboard is absorbent, you will need to apply at least two coats of primer.*

Paper and card

The cheapest support of all is paper. It can be used untreated for quick sketches, to work out ideas or to practise techniques. Because it is so absorbent, the paint surface will become very dry in time, but this does not matter for study pieces. A quick coat of size or acrylic primer will provide a more resistant surface. Prepare some sheets when you have a spare moment, so that you always have something to paint on. Good-quality wallpaper and cardboard are also excellent painting surfaces. Cut up cardboard boxes and save sheets of card packing. I've primed a piece of cardboard with an emulsion-glaze-emulsion-paint primer, but any acrylic primer or even a couple of coats of acrylic undercoat would also work.

Hardboard

This is an excellent support. It is relatively cheap, available in large sheets which can be cut down to the size that you want and provides two different surfaces, one with a rough, woven surface and the other smooth. It is tough and resilient, but the edges are weak and break easily. They can be protected by attaching battens, but generally only the largest sizes need to be treated in this way.

Hardboard, like canvas, needs to be sealed. Start by roughening the surface of the smooth side to give it some tooth – use coarse sandpaper or scrape the surface with an old sawblade. Then size both sides of the board; this prevents warping. When it is dry, apply an oil primer to the side you intend to use. Hardboard can also be sealed with an acrylic ground, but again apply the ground to both sides.

The rough side of hardboard is extremely absorbent and difficult to work and will wear out your brushes very quickly. Apply several coats of primer to provide a good seal and a surface which is easier to work and kinder to your brushes. It is worth experimenting with different grounds and treatments to see if you can work with hardboard; many artists use nothing else.

Applying fabric to hardboard

You can create cheap and interesting supports by covering hardboard with fine materials like muslin or scrim. Both are cheap, loosely woven cotton fabrics. Muslin is very fine and a pale cream in colour. Scrim is much coarser, has a more obvious texture and is a tawny-brown colour. Either can be applied to board with a coat of size or acrylic primer, which will act as both sealant and glue. Scrimmed or muslined boards have a good, interesting texture.

△ **Applying muslin to hardboard** *Muslin applied to hardboard provides an excellent surface with a good texture. I've used acrylic primer to seal and fix the muslin, but you could also use glue size. Start by cutting a piece of hardboard to the required size.*

▽ *Lay the hardboard on the muslin and cut a piece of muslin, allowing about a 2-in (5-cm) overlap all round. Now lay the muslin on top of the board, which should be smooth side uppermost as this is less absorbent. Flatten the muslin out and make sure the weave runs parallel to the edge of the board. Apply primer with a decorating brush, working from the centre and brushing outwards, smoothing out creases and bubbles as you work.*

▽ *Turn the board over, fold the muslin in and smooth down the flaps with a brush loaded with primer. Leave to dry. If you like a smooth finish, apply another coat of primer when the first is dry.*

▷ **Applying scrim to hardboard** *You will need scrim, a piece of hardboard cut to size and some prepared glue size.*

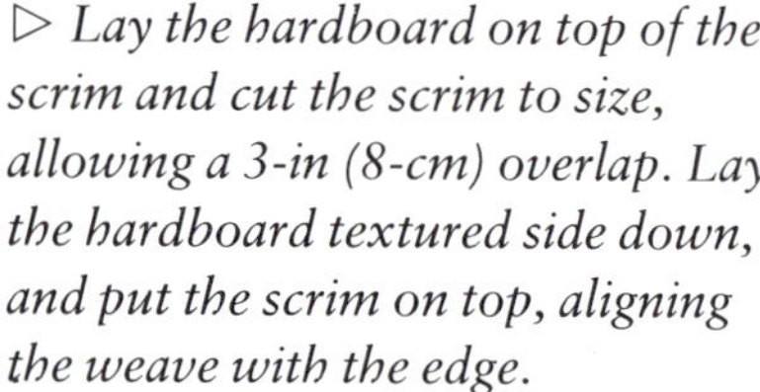

▷ *Lay the hardboard on top of the scrim and cut the scrim to size, allowing a 3-in (8-cm) overlap. Lay the hardboard textured side down, and put the scrim on top, aligning the weave with the edge.*

▽ *Pour warm size on to the scrim and work it over the surface using a large brush. Work out from the centre, smoothing out the wrinkles.*

▽ *Turn the board over, fold in the flaps of scrim and paste them down.*

Applying gesso to hardboard

Gesso is a ground made of gypsum or chalk mixed with water or size to provide a dense, brilliantly white surface traditionally used for egg tempera (pigment mixed or tempered with egg yolk) or some types of oil painting. The gesso was applied in a series of layers which were allowed to dry, then sanded down between applications and built up to a hard, white surface. Gesso powder is available from most artists' suppliers, and gessoed boards can be bought from specialist suppliers. Because it is so absorbent, a true gessoed ground requires a special approach, but it is worth experimenting to see if you like it. It is ideal for some kinds of detailed, small-scale work such as natural history subjects.

These days an acrylic gesso primer is widely available. This has the matt-white quality of a true gesso but is less absorbent and, because it is supplied ready-mixed, it is much simpler to prepare a board. It can also be used on canvas and paper.

△ *Cut the hardboard to the correct size and roughen the smooth side with sandpaper to give it some tooth. Apply the gesso primer, using a loaded decorator's brush. Work from side to side, using smooth, regular brushstrokes.*

▽ **Applying gesso primer to hardboard** *You can make a true gesso ground by buying gesso powder and mixing it with glue size, following the manufacturer's instructions. Acrylic gesso can be purchased ready-made and is much easier to use.*

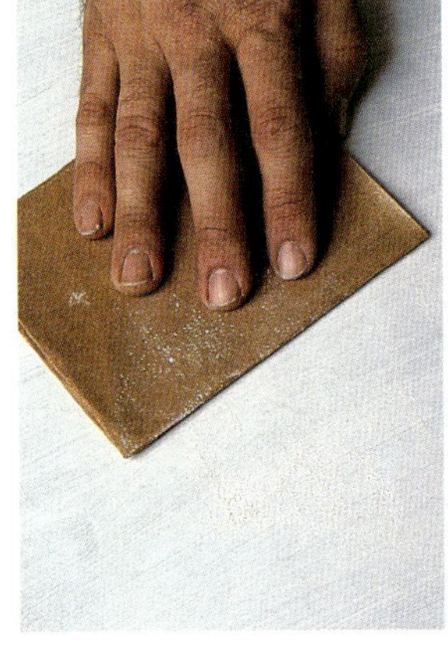

△ *Allow the primer to dry thoroughly, then sand the surface gently to get it smooth.*

△ *Apply another coat of primer, this time working at right angles to the first coat. Allow it to dry and repeat the process.*

CHAPTER 3 CHAPTER

Paints and Other Materials

THE TOOLS AND techniques of the oil painter have not changed much in the past 500 years and in that time has evolved a wonderfully arcane language, mysterious to the uninitiated but creating a bond between those within the magic circle. I love words like scumble and tonking, and the marvellously exotic oil of spike lavender, sun-bleached linseed oil and Venice turpentine. Indeed, one of the many pleasures of oil painting is pottering around art shops, leafing through specialist magazines and manufacturers' catalogues, and visiting craft and artists' materials exhibitions.

A first visit to an artists' materials supplier can be daunting for the beginner and so in this chapter I introduce the basic materials and explain the most useful terms. It is a good idea to develop a relationship with a particular shop. You'll find people in the trade are helpful and knowledgeable, and because many of them are practising artists in their spare time, they are happy to talk about painting, materials and your particular requirements.

Artists' materials are enjoyable for their own sake. In time you'll find out which you like best, developing your own collection of old favourites.

PAINTS AND PIGMENTS

A pigment is a solid coloured substance which is ground to create a powder. Some pigments occur naturally; others are manufactured in a chemical process. Because pure pigment in powder form cannot be made to stick to a support, pigments are mixed with a binding medium to create a paint. Different binding media are used for different types of paint: the binding medium for oil paint is linseed oil; that for watercolour is gum arabic. You can buy pigment powder and make your own paint, but although some artists remain convinced that hand-ground pigments are superior to tube colours, stick to ready-made paints to start with. Different types of paint are referred to as media, so oil, watercolour and acrylic are all media. Drawing materials like pencil, pastel and coloured pencil are also described as media.

Earth pigments

Pigments can be divided into groups which reflect their origins and method of manufacture. The earth colours are a large group of naturally occurring pigments which include yellow ochre, raw sienna, burnt sienna, raw umber, burnt umber, light red, Venetian red and terre verte. Earth colours have been used since prehistoric times and there are surviving examples of cave paintings made with these materials at various sites in Spain and France, such as Altamira and Lascaux. These paintings, which are about 20,000 years old, show bison, running deer and boar, the animals our forebears hunted and lived by, and are rendered vigorously and confidently. The palaeolithic artists used materials which they found about them – naturally occurring earths, ochres, manganese oxides, charcoal and iron carbonates, which gave various shades of red and yellow as well as black. Whites, greens and blues are not found at these sites. The pigments were collected, ground to a powder, mixed with melted fat and applied to the walls with brushes, fingers, twigs, feathers or leaves.

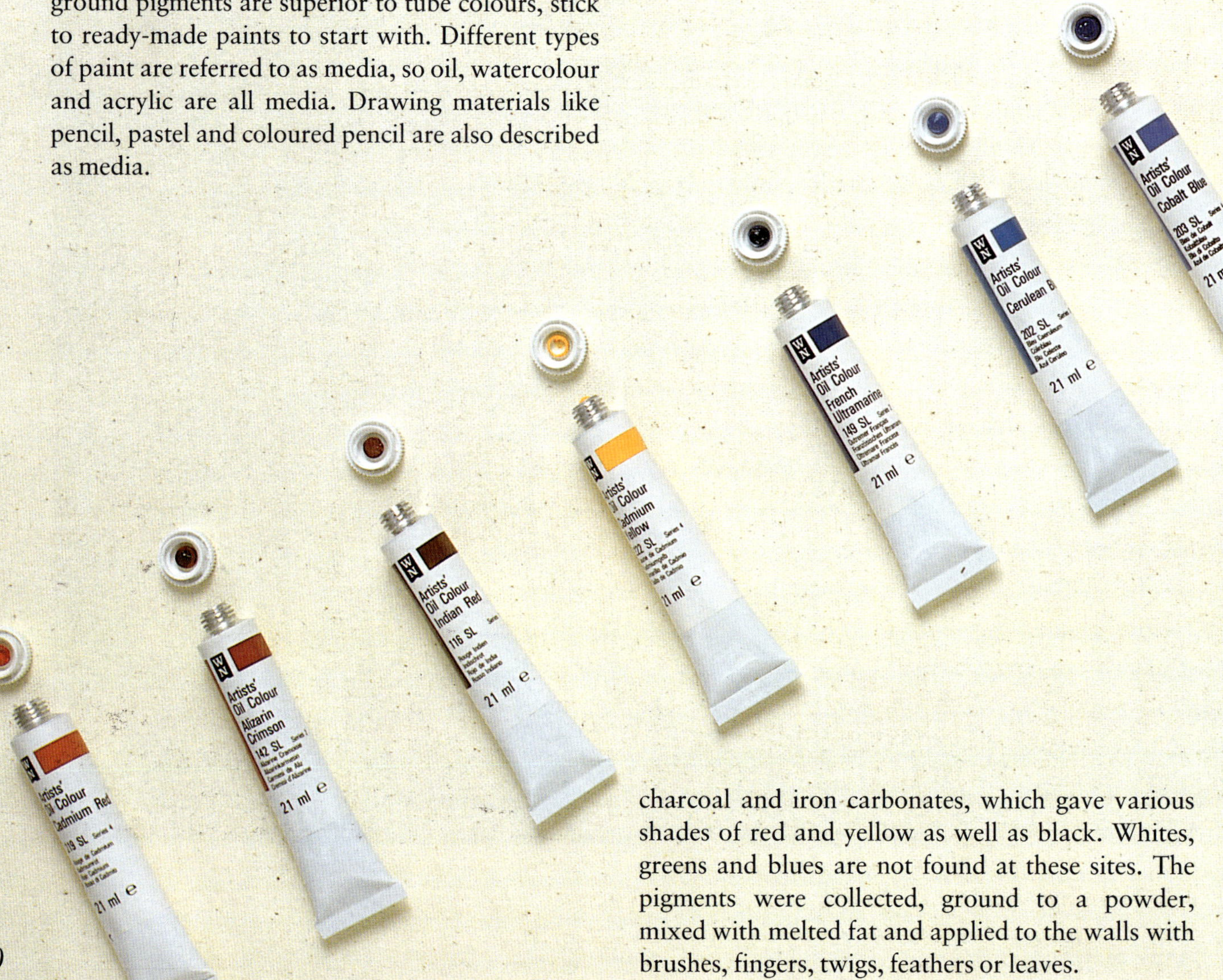

Organic and inorganic pigments
Inorganic pigments like viridian and cobalt blue are produced chemically. Organic pigments like rose madder and the 'lake' colours are extracted from raw materials in the form of a dye which must then be mixed with a substrate, such as alumina, so that when dry they can be ground.

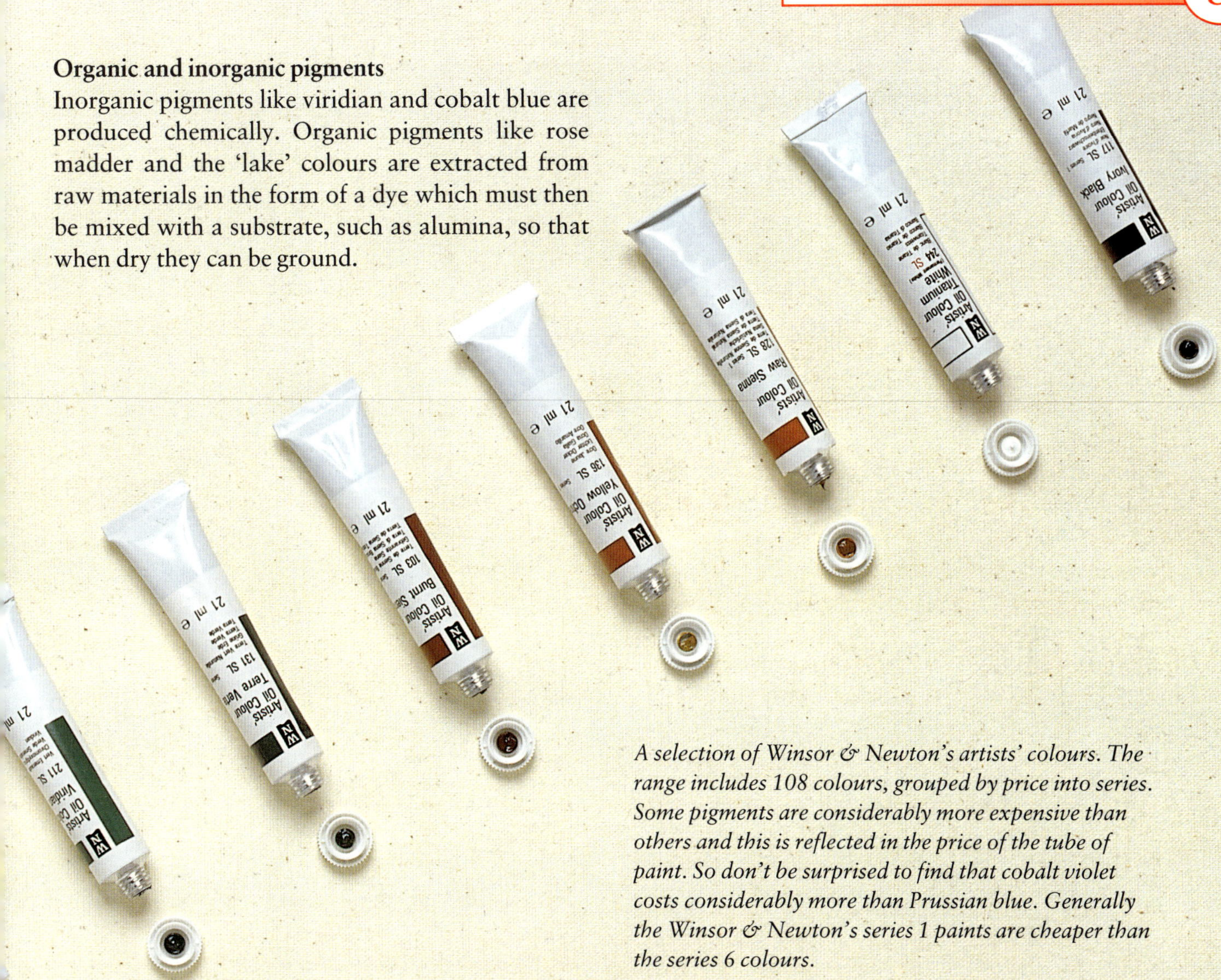

A selection of Winsor & Newton's artists' colours. The range includes 108 colours, grouped by price into series. Some pigments are considerably more expensive than others and this is reflected in the price of the tube of paint. So don't be surprised to find that cobalt violet costs considerably more than Prussian blue. Generally the Winsor & Newton's series 1 paints are cheaper than the series 6 colours.

Artists' or students' quality
Oil paint is sold in tubes and most manufacturers produce two ranges: artists' and students' quality. The former contains the best pigments and has the highest proportion of pigment to extender. The latter cost less and the range of colours is more limited. For example, while Winsor & Newton have 108 colours in their artists' range, there are only forty-seven in their students' range. The price of an individual colour largely depends on the cost of the raw material used and some colours are available only in the artists' range. Costs are kept down by replacing some of the more expensive and traditional pigments with modern alternatives. Students' colours lack some of the finer qualities of the artists' range, but you won't notice this to start with and they are good value for the beginner.

Permanence
Some colours are more permanent than others, and paint manufacturers have a coding system which indicates the degree of permanence of a particular colour. These codes are clearly printed on the tube and you will find the key to them in the manufacturers' catalogue or in leaflets. Although permanence will not concern you at this stage, it may become relevant later on. For example, if you eventually work to commission, you will want to be sure that your colours will not deteriorate or fade.

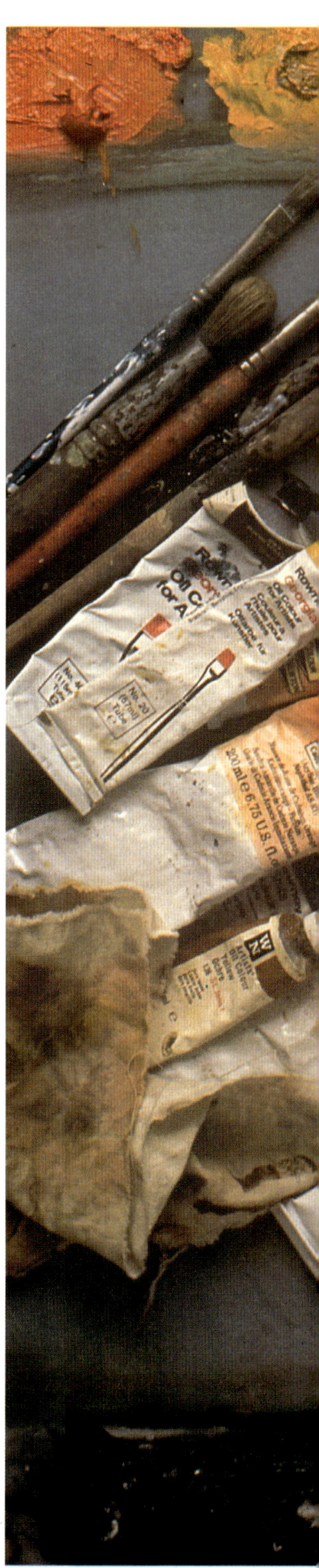

△ **Get to know colours** *Collect manufacturers' colour charts. They will help you become familiar with the names and appearance of colours and are a useful reference when reordering paints. Collect samples of canvas as well.*

Catalogues and colour charts

Manufacturers' catalogues are a mine of information so it is worth collecting and studying them. You generally have to pay for them, but not very much. Not only do they show you what is on the market but they also contain a great deal of useful technical information.

Most paint manufacturers, also known as artists' colourmen, produce printed colour charts which illustrate and name their entire range of colours, and give a product code number for reordering. These printed charts are a guide only; the limitations of the printing process prevent absolute accuracy. Many colourmen also produce charts made with washes of paint. These are handmade and therefore costly to produce, but they are a valuable tool and will prove extremely useful.

Looking after paints

Paints are costly, so look after them. Always put the cap on when you have finished. To make sure it goes on properly, wipe the neck and the inside of the lid with a cloth that has a little turpentine or

▽ **Care of paints** *Clean excess paint from the top of the tube with a rag. This will ensure that the lid screws on properly.*

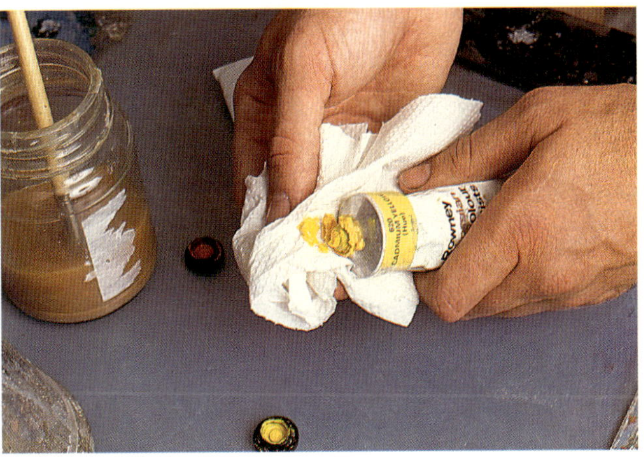

◁ *Look after your materials. Clean brushes after every session and put the lids back on the tubes of paint.*

white spirit on it. This will keep the threads clean and ensure a good seal. It should also prevent the cap getting stuck, although if this does happen, try freeing it with pliers, or grip it in the door jamb. Running hot water over the lid sometimes does the trick.

Keep the outside of your tubes clean. This might sound rather prissy but there is nothing more irritating than having a tube of colour which is so grubby that the name of the colour is obliterated. You have to waste time unscrewing the lid and squeezing out colour to see it, and if you like a colour you'll need to know what it is in order to get some more.

DILUENTS AND MEDIA

There are many products which can be added to oil paint to change its consistency and texture, the way that it moves over the support, the way it holds the mark of the brush and the speed with which it dries.

Diluents

A diluent is a solvent which thins the paint so that it can be mixed and handled more easily, but it evaporates completely and has no binding effect on the pigment. Turpentine is the most useful and popular solvent for oil painting. Made from the distilled resin of pine trees, it is a clear, volatile, flammable liquid with a characteristic smell. It speeds up the drying time of the oils used to bind the pigments in the paint, and also the media you add. Turpentine should stored in the dark, in tightly sealed containers, as exposure to air and light causes it to become thick and treacly.

Shown here are a selection of painting media. Turpentine is the most common diluent used with oil paint. Winsor & Newton's Liquin is an extremely useful alkyd medium developed to increase the flow and speed the drying time of oil paint. Linseed oil increases the flow and transparency of oil paint. Wingel is a quick-drying glazing medium. Oleopasto is a translucent gel which can be used to extend the paint and to build up impasto textures.

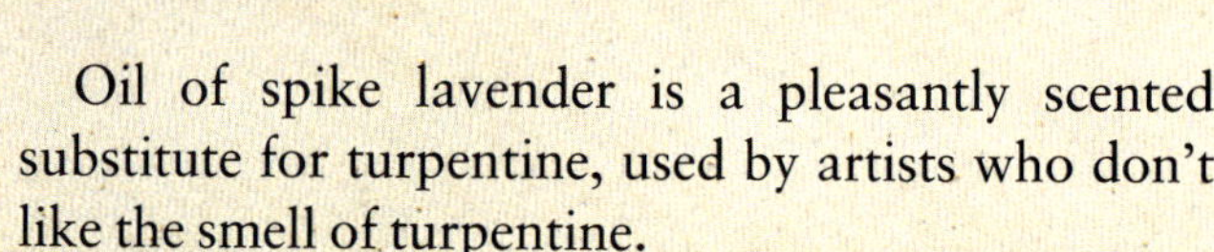

Oil of spike lavender is a pleasantly scented substitute for turpentine, used by artists who don't like the smell of turpentine.

The other solvent used with oil paint is turpentine substitute or white spirit. This is considerably cheaper than turpentine, but it is impure and should not be used for painting. However, it is ideal for cleaning brushes and palettes, so you should always have plenty to hand.

Media

A medium is anything you add to paint to change its character and the way it handles. By adding a medium you can, for example, thin a paint to make it less opaque in order to create transparent glazes of colour. Another medium will give the paint more substance so that it holds the mark of the brush or knife, allowing you to build up a thick impasto. Media can be added to accelerate the drying time –

useful if you are working out of doors or want to lay a series of glazes. Others will slow the rate at which the paint dries; this could be useful if you work slowly and want to use a wet-into-wet technique, rather than painting wet on top of dry paint.

Drying oils

The oils which are added to oil paint to change the way it behaves are called drying oils. The most popular oil medium used with oil paint is linseed oil. That sounds simple enough, but when you go to your art supplier to buy some, you'll be faced with a whole range of different types of linseed oil.

Refined linseed oil will do to start with. It is a pale oil which thins oil colour, increases gloss and transparency, and reduces the rate at which the paint dries.

The best-quality linseed oil, called cold-pressed linseed oil, is extracted from flax seeds without heat. The process produces less oil and the product is therefore more expensive. Other forms of linseed oil have slightly different qualities and properties. For example, sun-bleached linseed oil dries slightly faster than refined linseed oil, while standard linseed oil slows drying but gives the paint surface a tough, elastic finish, and drying linseed oil increases the rate at which the paint dries.

The other common oil medium is poppy oil. Like linseed oil, it is used to bind dry pigments into a paint in the manufacturing process. Because poppy oils are pale, they are often used with whites and pale colours in situations when it is important not to darken the paint.

Most manufacturers produce a range of traditional oil media made from the various mixtures of oils and solvents. Each has specific qualities. Look around each time you visit your artists' materials supplier, pick up leaflets and look at catalogues. In time you'll become familiar with the ranges.

The alkyd media

In the last twenty years manufacturers have developed a range of alkyd-resin-based media. These are generally characterized by their fast drying times but, like the oil media, each has different qualities.

In time you will get around to experimenting with all these different media, but for the time being keep things simple and stick to refined linseed oil and possibly one of the alkyd media to allow you to work quickly.

▷ *Hog-hair brushes, from left to right: round, flat, filbert, bright, fan.*

▽ *Synthetic/hair-blend brushes, from top to bottom: flat, four round brushes, rigger.*

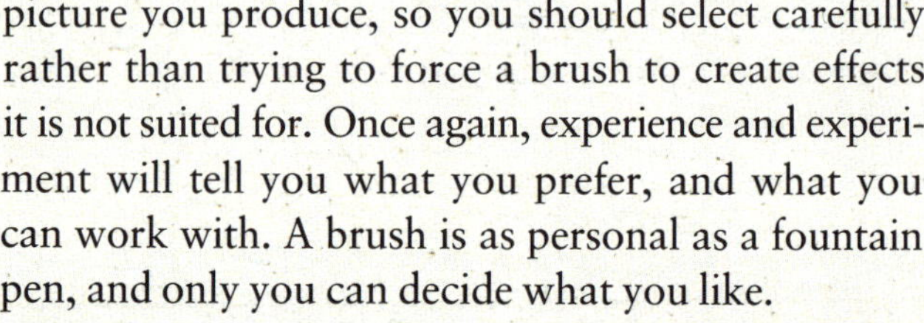

BRUSHES AND KNIVES

Brights, filberts, flats and fans, hog, sable and ox – and you only wanted a brush! Even the smallest art shop will have a large selection of brushes in different sizes, shapes and materials, and at wildly different prices.

Brushes are important. They are the artist's principal tool for applying paints to a support, and over the centuries the very best shape and quality for every task has been evolved. The kind of brush you use will make a great difference to the kind of picture you produce, so you should select carefully rather than trying to force a brush to create effects it is not suited for. Once again, experience and experiment will tell you what you prefer, and what you can work with. A brush is as personal as a fountain pen, and only you can decide what you like.

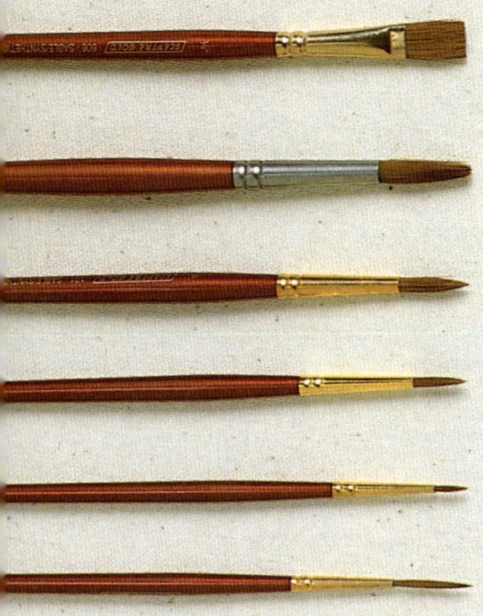

Brushes for oil painting have long handles, because generally you will be working at an easel, at a distance from the support. A long handle is good for large-scale work because it encourages you to work more broadly and freely from the elbow and the shoulder, rather than from the wrist. Watercolour brushes have shorter handles, but if you do small-scale oils you might prefer to use short-handled brushes.

Types of Brush

Three types of brush are used by the oil painter: natural bristle, natural hair or synthetic fibre, which simulates the characteristics of the first two.

The most popular oil-painting brushes are hog hair, which are made from pigs' bristle. Each strand of bristle has split ends, or flags, which allow the brush to hold a large quantity of paint. Bristle brushes are stiff and hard-wearing, qualities which make them ideally suited to the stiff texture and coarser grounds used for oil paint.

There are four main shapes for oil painting: round, flat, bright and filbert. Round brushes are useful for applying thinned paint to large areas and for painting lines. Flats have long bristles and can be used for laying on bold, broad areas of colour; the sides can be used to make lines and short marks.

Brights are like flats but have shorter bristles; they are useful for more controlled work. Filberts are similar to flats but curve inwards at the ends; they are very useful and can be used for tapering strokes and dabs of colour. Then there are fan brushes, designed for detailed work such as rendering hair, and riggers, which are long, very thin brushes with a fine point designed for line work and lettering.

The best hog brushes are handmade, with the bundles of bristles bound together in such a way that the natural curves of each filament points inward to give the brush a neat profile.

Sable brushes are ideal for glazes and fine work. Those with long handles are designed for oil painting. The very finest sable is made from the tail hair of the wild mink, a weasel from the cold regions of Siberia and Korea. This is a costly and fairly rare material, so if you do invest in a good sable brush, treat it with care.

Other soft-hair brushes are made from mixed fibres including ox hair, sable and synthetic materials. The synthetic materials have improved considerably in recent years and these make ideal and moderately priced alternatives to sable.

Brush sizes

Brushes are generally sold in a range of sizes marked from 00, the smallest, to 14. However, a 14 in one range will be different from a 14 in another. You'll find a larger brush useful for tinting canvases and laying in broad underpaintings. Start with a 2-in (5-cm) decorator's brush.

Choosing a brush

When selecting a brush, get the best you can afford, and buy a few good brushes rather than lots of cheap ones. Choose brushes that look neat and don't have stray hairs sticking out at odd angles. Test the springiness of the brush by pressing it gently, tip down, in the palm of your hand. Soft hair brushes should spring back into shape when wet. Test this by dipping them in water to see that they hold their shape. Good art shops provide a pot of water for this purpose.

Knives

There are two types of knives used for oil painting. Palette knives have flat, broad, flexible steel blades and wooden handles. They are used for mixing paint and cleaning palettes. Painting knives, on the other hand, are designed for applying paint and have flexible steel blades in a range of shapes,

▽ *Hog-hair brushes, from left to right: filbert, bright, flat, round.*

◁ *Left: painting knife. Right: palette knife.*

generally triangular with a pointed end. Between the blade and the wooden handle there is a cranked shaft which allows you to work on the canvas. To confuse the issue, 'painting' knives are used for a technique which is called 'palette knife' painting. Painting knives allow you to build up a thick impasto, which looks quite different from that achieved with the brush.

Care of brushes

Brushes are costly and essential tools, so they must be looked after. Always clean brushes immediately after use. Don't leave them standing bristle-end down in a jar of white spirit as the pressure will distort the hair. It is a good idea to use two jars of white spirit, one for getting the worst of the paint off, the other for a final rinse in clean fluid. Next hold the brush under cold water and rub it gently on a cake of soap. Then work the bristles in the palm of your hand so that you work up a lather. Clean the bristles right up to the ferrule. Rinse the brush in water, squeeze out excess water between

Cleaning brushes

▽ **1** *Start by wiping the brush on a piece of rag or kitchen towel. This will remove a lot of the paint.*

△ **4** *Moisten the brush in cold or warm (not hot) water.*

your fingers and gently pull the bristles back into shape. Soft-hair brushes can be brought back into shape with a vigorous flick of the wrist. Store brushes bristle-end up.

If you do allow paint to dry on your brush, you can clean it with a commercial brush cleaner, then wash it with water and soap to remove the solvent. These cleaners are fairly drastic, so avoid letting your brushes get into this state.

▽ **2** *Dip the brush in a jar of white spirit and move it about vigorously. If there is a lot of paint near the ferrule, press the brush against the base of the jar.*

▽ **3** *Wipe the brush on a rag. You should have removed most of the paint, but if the brush is large or heavily loaded you may have to dip it in white spirit again.*

△ **5** *Rub the bristles gently on a bar of soap, then work them around the palm of your hand.*

△ **6** *Work up a lather: you need to loosen all the paint, especially around the ferrule.*

△ **7** *Rinse the brush under running water, making sure you remove all the soap.*

EASELS

An easel will be one of your most expensive outlays, but a good one will last a lifetime and it is difficult to paint in oil without one. There are many different kinds of easel and the type you choose will depend on where you paint, what scale you work on and what you can afford.

Portable easels

If you intend to work out of doors regularly, you will need a portable easel. Even though with a bit of ingenuity you can probably find some way of propping up your work, painting is difficult enough without having to contend with a canvas which keeps slipping about, or gets blown away by the wind. The cheapest type of easel is a folding wooden sketching easel. These are light, take canvases or boards up to about 50 in (127 cm) square and can be fixed either upright, or horizontal for watercolour sketching. Because the easels are compact when folded, they are easy to carry and store. A good sketching easel is a sensible investment if you don't want to spend a lot of money, and don't have a great deal of space for work or storage.

Another version of the sketching easel is made in aluminium. Like the wooden easel, it is compact when folded and can also take a canvas of up to about 50 in (127 cm) square. Aluminium easels are slightly more stable and easier to erect than wooden ones, but are also rather more expensive. However, they are ideal for sketching and a useful compromise for working at home.

Easel boxes

The easel sketch box is one of those wonderfully well-designed products that have evolved over a period of time to meet a particular need. They are tripod easels with a drawer for paints, palette and brushes. They fold down to a box, with a carrying handle and clips which can hold one small, wet canvas. Do have look at them. They are intriguing and, though expensive, ideal if you paint away from home a great deal. After dropping a lot of hints, I was given one as a present and love it.

Big easels

Next we step up to bigger easels, definitely not portable but very stable and designed to take large canvases. Radial easels have short tripod legs, can be tilted backwards and forwards and take canvases up to about 76 in (193 cm) square. They can be folded for storage.

Studio easels have firm H-shaped bases and a ledge for brushes. They can be tilted backwards and forwards, and the canvas can be raised or lowered by means of a catch or ratchet. Some studio easels fold flat, but they still take up more space than a radial easel.

Artists' donkey

This traditional design combines a drawing-board support and a bench on which the artist can sit astride. Some donkeys have a bench with storage space. Both are popular in schools and art colleges.

How to choose

The price of these various styles of easel depends on the material from which they are made, their size, and the quality of the craftsmanship. Good hardwoods such as mahogany are the most expensive, but excellent and much cheaper easels are made in softwoods. Treat the easel with linseed oil before you use it. This will feed the wood and give it a protective seal. The easel will become spattered with paint in time. This doesn't matter, but do make sure that the hinges and bolts remain free by keeping them clean and treating them with a lubricating oil from time to time. Wipe an oily rag over the wood every so often too.

An easel is an important purchase so take your time, talk to other painters and have a look around before you buy.

▷ Left to right: a standard radial easel; a bench easel, with storage; a jointed radial easel, which can be used horizontal for watercolour, vertical for oils.

△ *A sturdy, good quality studio easel will be fairly expensive. However, it is wonderful to have a steady, vertical surface to work on, so that you can step back to see the painting progressing.*

OTHER EQUIPMENT

Palettes

Palettes are the surface on which an artist mixes colours. Traditionally, palettes for oil painting are oval, rectangular or kidney-shaped boards made of lightweight hardwood, such as mahogany. They have a thumbhole so that they can be supported on one arm, allowing you to carry your colours as you move backwards and forwards in front of the easel. A good palette should be well balanced and comfortable to hold. To clean your palette, which you will need to do from time to time, scrape off surplus paint with a palette knife, wipe the board with turpentine, then oil it with linseed oil. In time the board will build up a rich, protective patina.

You can make a palette from plywood or any other cheap wood. Sand the wood to get a smooth finish, then seal it by painting it with a layer of linseed oil. Wipe off the excess with paper towels or a rag, and leave it to dry for several days. Apply another coat of linseed oil, allow that to dry and repeat the process until you have a good hard seal.

Some artists prefer not to carry their palette but walk to it. Many convert a trolley by fixing a wood, glass or melamine surface on to it, thus giving themselves a much larger mixing surface which can be wheeled about the studio, with storage space for various media, paints and rags below.

Choose a palette larger than you think you will need. This will give you plenty of space for mixing colour and experimenting. If your palette is too small, you will quickly run out of space and this will artificially limit your opportunities for exploration and investigation. To begin with you will inevitably spend a great deal of time looking for the right colours.

Peel-off palettes are available on paper pads. They are handy if you are working outside as they can be thrown away once you're finished, but they are too expensive for everyday use and too small to be really serviceable.

Dippers, pots and jars

You will need containers for the diluents and media you mix with your paint. Dippers are metal containers that clip to the palette, so that the media are near the paints for mixing. They are available in different sizes, singly and in pairs, with lids and without. Those with tops prevent the medium drying out, so that you can keep them for quite a long time – useful if you work slowly and need only small amounts. If you paint larger pictures and use lots of media, you'll probably end up with a collection of jars, saucers and dishes in which to put ready-mixed media, and for mixing your own.

Artists are inveterate collectors of glass jars. You'll need at least two for brush-cleaning and another for storing brushes. Nor can you have

Traditional mahogany kidney-shaped palettes, a rectangular birch ply palette, a double dipper, putty rubbers, cartridge sketch pads and a selection of willow charcoal.

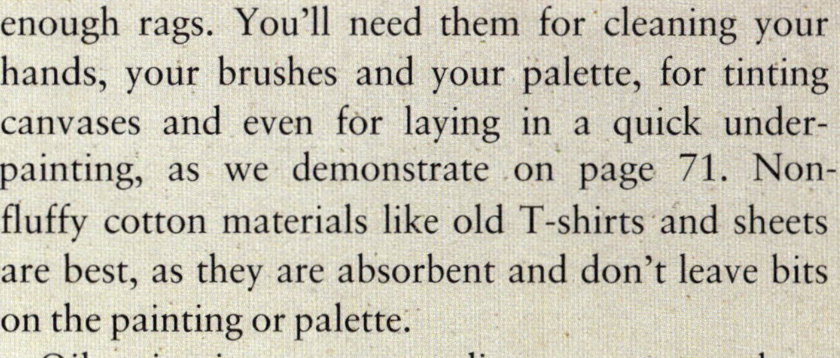

enough rags. You'll need them for cleaning your hands, your brushes and your palette, for tinting canvases and even for laying in a quick under-painting, as we demonstrate on page 71. Non-fluffy cotton materials like old T-shirts and sheets are best, as they are absorbent and don't leave bits on the painting or palette.

Oil paint is a messy medium, no matter how careful you are. It is sticky and takes ages to dry, so a wet canvas is a hazard for days, if not weeks. In an ideal world you would have a room just for painting and then you could leave your palette of colours and wet paintings between sessions. However, if, like most people, you have to pack your things away when you finish painting, make sure they are stored well out of the way. If not, you'll find that oil paint gets everywhere.

Other essentials for the oil painter are kitchen roll, an overall and lots of newspaper for mopping up spills, protecting surfaces and tonking – I explain tonking later (see page 51).

Drawing materials

You will need a sketchbook to make preparatory drawing in pencil or charcoal. Charcoal is particularly useful for quick tonal studies and also for underdrawing, as it can be dusted off leaving only a faint outline. Willow charcoal is the nicest to use. It is soft, offers a narrow tip for linear work and the long edge can be used for blocking in areas of solid tone. Willow charcoal is available in thin, medium or thick sticks, and sometimes in assorted widths. Charcoal pencils are cleaner, but the charcoal is harder and they lack willow's sweet, fluid quality.

A putty rubber can be moulded to a fine point so that you can erase small areas and pick out highlights without smearing – particularly useful when you are working with charcoal.

CHAPTER 4 CHAPTER

Colour

COLOUR CONCERNS all painters no matter what medium they work in. It is one of the primary means by which they describe the world and express their responses to it. No artist ever claims to have mastered colour; it is something they continue to learn about and experiment with throughout their working lives.

Colour is a vast and confusing subject, the study of which covers many disciplines. Physicists study the phenomenon of light, chemists look at the properties of dyes and pigments, physiologists study the way the eye and brain allow us to perceive and interpret colour, while psychologists seek to understand its symbolism and the way we respond to it.

Artists can use the findings of all these disciplines, but more importantly they must learn to 'see' colour. Having trained themselves to see it, they must then learn to handle their medium so that with solid and relatively crude materials in a finite range of colours they can re-create subtle and infinitely varied light effects. It's quite a challenge. But above all colour is a pleasure, something to be played with and enjoyed.

In this painting the artist, Lionel Bulmer, takes an everyday subject – an oval table with a patterned cloth – and by flattening form and editing and exaggerating colour creates an image which is unique and exciting.

Using colour

There are two principal ways in which artists use colour. The constructive use of colour renders three-dimensional space and form on a two-dimensional surface. Artists use colour to construct an illusion. In aerial perspective, for example, they make use of the way that cool colours appear to recede while warm colours advance. Colour can also be used to express emotions, mood and atmosphere, and generate an emotional response in the viewer.

Seeing colour

You can't paint colour until you learn to see it. But when you start to look with the eye of an artist you'll realize that the world we live in is more colourful than you had previously thought. Take shadows, for example. Children and naïve painters paint shadows as though they were black or dark grey, but if you look hard you will see that they are full of subtle colour and tone. If light really did travel only in straight lines from its source, the areas of an object which are cut off from the direct rays of the sun would indeed be pure black. But in fact the sun's rays are scattered and reflected back from the surface they strike, creating a shimmering, complex and constantly changing background light. Even in a brightly lit landscape, shadows are not pure black but are softly modulated, tinged with colour from surrounding objects and the sky above.

The colour wheel

One of the devices by which artists try to understand colour is the colour wheel. This is a circular diagram used to show how colours can be mixed from the three primaries, and it explains certain colour relationships.

Let's look at the primaries: red, yellow and blue. These are important because they cannot be mixed on the palette from other colours, and in theory every other colour can be mixed from them.

Orange, green and violet are called the secondaries because they are derived from the primaries: red and yellow produce orange; yellow and blue produce green; and red and blue produce violet.

▷ This colour wheel shows primary and secondary colours, with warms on one side, cools on the other and complementaries opposite each other.

The tertiaries are produced by adding a primary to a secondary. They produce useful colours like bluish green and yellowy green, reddish orange and reddish violet.

Definitions

Colour has its own vocabulary and it will be helpful to understand some of the terms. Every colour has four qualities: hue, tone (or value), intensity (or saturation) and temperature.

A hue is a specific colour, defined in terms of its redness or blueness, but not its lightness or darkness.

Tone is the lightness or darkness of a colour. White and black represent the two extremes of the tonal scale and any colour can be placed somewhere in between.

The effect of adding black, white or grey to a hue is to reduce its intensity. The colours around the outside of the colour wheel are at their maximum intensity because they cannot be made any stronger. They can, however, be broken down into weaker forms, by adding white, black or grey, while still retaining their hue.

Temperature refers to the degree of warmth or coldness of a colour. This is a subjective and aesthetic distinction which has no physical basis, but it is invaluable to the artist. In the projects later in the book I constantly refer to warm and cool colours.

Warm and cool colours

The colour circle can be divided into two halves. In one we find the warm colours: yellows, reds and oranges. In the other are the cool colours: blues, violets and greens. But there are degrees of warmth and coolness, so some blues are relatively warm and some reds are relatively cool. Ultramarine, for example, is a warm blue that can be mixed with red to make a good violet. Prussian blue, on the other hand, is a cool blue and can be mixed with a 'cool' yellow like lemon yellow to give a brilliant green. Study a colour chart and you will see that reds like carmine and alizarin crimson are cooler than hot reds like cadmium red and scarlet.

Generally, warm and cool colours are carefully orchestrated to create a picture that appears neither too cold nor too hot. However, in painting rules are often broken for creative effect, and a painter may deliberately pitch a painting in a warm or cool key.

Aerial perspective

While warm colours appear to advance towards the spectator, cool colours seem to recede. Aerial or colour perspective is a device by which the artist creates an illusion of space using cool colours in the background and warm colours in the foreground. If you look at objects in the distance, you will see that the further away they are the less distinct they become – edges become blurred and colours and tones move closer together. By blurring forms, using cool and muted colours in the background, and contrasting this with crisp edges, bright and warm colours in the foreground, you can enhance the sense of space in your work.

Complementary colours

These are pairs of colours that are opposite each other on the colour wheel. Take the primaries, for example. Every primary colour has a complementary which is a mixture of the other two primaries. Study the colour wheel and you will see that orange (red plus yellow) is the complementary of blue; green (yellow plus blue) the complementary of red; and violet (blue plus red) the complementary of yellow. Complementary colours have a special relationship. When placed side by side they intensify each other, so red looks redder when it is juxtaposed with green. For a practical application, study the work of the Impressionist painters. You will find that almost invariably areas of green like grass and trees have traces of their complementary reds, giving the greens a special zest and vividness. If you mix two complementaries, you will create a neutral brown or grey – useful, subtle shades that are more interesting than the greys produced by mixing white and black.

Looking for tones

We have already defined the term tone (or value) as the lightness or darkness of a colour. Just as we learn to see colour, so we also learn to see tone. It is the distribution of lights and darks over the surface of an object that allows us to understand its form. Look at any subject while ignoring the local colour – the actual colour of an object or an area – and try to see it purely in terms of lights and darks. Half closing your eyes will help by emphasizing the contrasts. A black-and-white photograph is a good example of a tonal study.

Get into the habit of making a tonal study of a subject before you paint it. Charcoal is an ideal medium for this because it is capable of rendering subtle tonal gradations. A tonal study will do two things. It will both help you to understand the forms and also let you see very clearly an important aspect of the composition, the distribution of lights and darks across the picture area. In a successful painting these will be arranged in a balanced and harmonious way.

A useful way of learning about composition is to make tonal studies of the works of great artists. Take your sketchbook to an art gallery and look at your favourite pictures, or find reproductions in books. Study the paintings through half-closed eyes so that you can identify the dark masses and the light areas. Make quick, scribbled drawings of these lights and darks. The results will be sketchy, almost abstract images. By studying these, you will learn a great deal about the way these artists used the picture area.

▽ **Mixing colours for landscape**
Learning to mix colours is an essential part of the artist's training. Here I show some greens and greeny-browns that would be useful for a landscape painting. From left to right: raw sienna and viridian; viridian and cadmium yellow pale; cadmium yellow pale and black; yellow ochre and French ultramarine; French ultramarine and raw sienna.

The colours here are, above, left to right: yellow ochre, burnt sienna, alizarin crimson, raw sienna, burnt umber, chrome orange, chrome yellow, ivory black and cadmium yellow. Below, left to right: Payne's Grey, cobalt blue, viridian, Prussian blue, cerulean blue, chrome green, French ultramarine, sap green.

CHAPTER 5 CHAPTER

Starting to Paint

OIL IS A wonderfully sensuous and responsive medium. To get the most out of it you should first learn to enjoy and feel comfortable with the materials and the paint. The basic oil techniques which I will describe in this chapter are actually very simple to follow. However, before you work through them I suggest you play with the paint for a while. Take two or three tubes of colour, a few sheets of primed paper or board, and a couple of brushes and just have a go.

Squeeze a blob of paint on to a palette, load a brush with paint and see how it moves on the support. Now see what happens when you use a smaller brush, a knife, a rag or your finger. Vary the amount of paint on your brush. See what effects you get with a heavily loaded brush, and then with a fairly dry brush. Thin the paint with a little turpentine and experiment with that. Notice whether it covers the board or whether the ground shows through. Does the paint retain the mark of the brush? Try mixing the paint with linseed oil and see what difference that makes. Get to know the paint: play with it and enjoy it. When you've finished, you can scrape the paint off with a palette knife, wipe the support with rag and turpentine and start again. Or you can allow your experiments to dry and paint over them with primer.

△ *Paint is used to create descriptive effects, but it can also give a picture surface character and energy. In this detail the paint surface is flat and unmodulated in some areas, but on the left layers of broken greens create a sense of flickering, moving colour, while on the right the artist has scratched back into the paint surface to suggest grasses.*

◁ *Tonking is a method of removing excess paint from the support. Lay a piece of absorbent paper over the area – newspaper will do – and rub it gently. Peel the paper off and you'll find that some of the paint comes too. Tonking is useful when the paint surface gets so wet and slippery that it is difficult to continue painting. The technique was devised by Henry Tonks.*

A BASIC KIT

If you are starting from scratch, you may find this shopping list of basic items useful. There are so many materials available that the novice sometimes doesn't know where to start. Once you've mastered the basic techniques described in this book, and worked through the projects, you will know your likes and dislikes and whether the medium suits you. This list is intended to get you started.

Buy some turpentine to thin the paint and lots of white spirit to clean your brushes. It might also be worth buying one of the alkyd mediums as these allow you to work quickly. I found Winsor & Newton's Wingel very useful for the projects in this book.

Make sure you have plenty of painting surfaces. A pad of oil sketching paper plus three or four canvas boards would be good to start with. The supports should be a reasonable size, otherwise you'll fiddle, and you should start by painting boldly and broadly to get the feel of the medium. The 24 in × 20 in (61 cm × 51 cm) or 30 in × 20 in (76 cm × 51 cm) sizes are good. Or you can buy hardboard. Cut it to these sizes and prime it with an acrylic primer.

You will need four or five brushes. Choose hog brushes and, as with the supports, pick ones that are slightly larger than you think you need. Sizes vary from manufacturer to manufacturer so I'll be specific and recommend the Winsor & Newton set which includes a number 4 flat, a number 6 filbert, a number 1 round and a number 8 bright. You'll also need a soft brush for underdrawing and putting in details – a number 3 synthetic or mixed fibre brush is good here.

A palette or mixing surface is essential. This can be bought or home-made, but make sure it is big enough. A sheet of glass or melamine board makes an excellent fixed palette.

Make sure you have lots of rags, kitchen towel and newspaper for protecting surfaces, cleaning and mopping up spills.

Paints

All colours are available in 21 ml and 37 ml tubes; whites can also be bought in 60 ml and 120 ml tubes. Choose the 37 ml size for most colours, but you'll need a 60 ml tube of white. Start with a few colours and add others as you become more knowledgeable and confident.

▽ Flesh tones
Start with this limited palette – later you will evolve your own.

A limited palette

The beginner is easily tempted into buying lots of colours, but this is both unnecessary and expensive. It is better to start with a limited range of colours. If you have only a few colours you will be forced to make the ones you need by mixing them and this means you will have to look hard and analyse just what it is you are seeing. In this way you will sharpen your perception of colour.

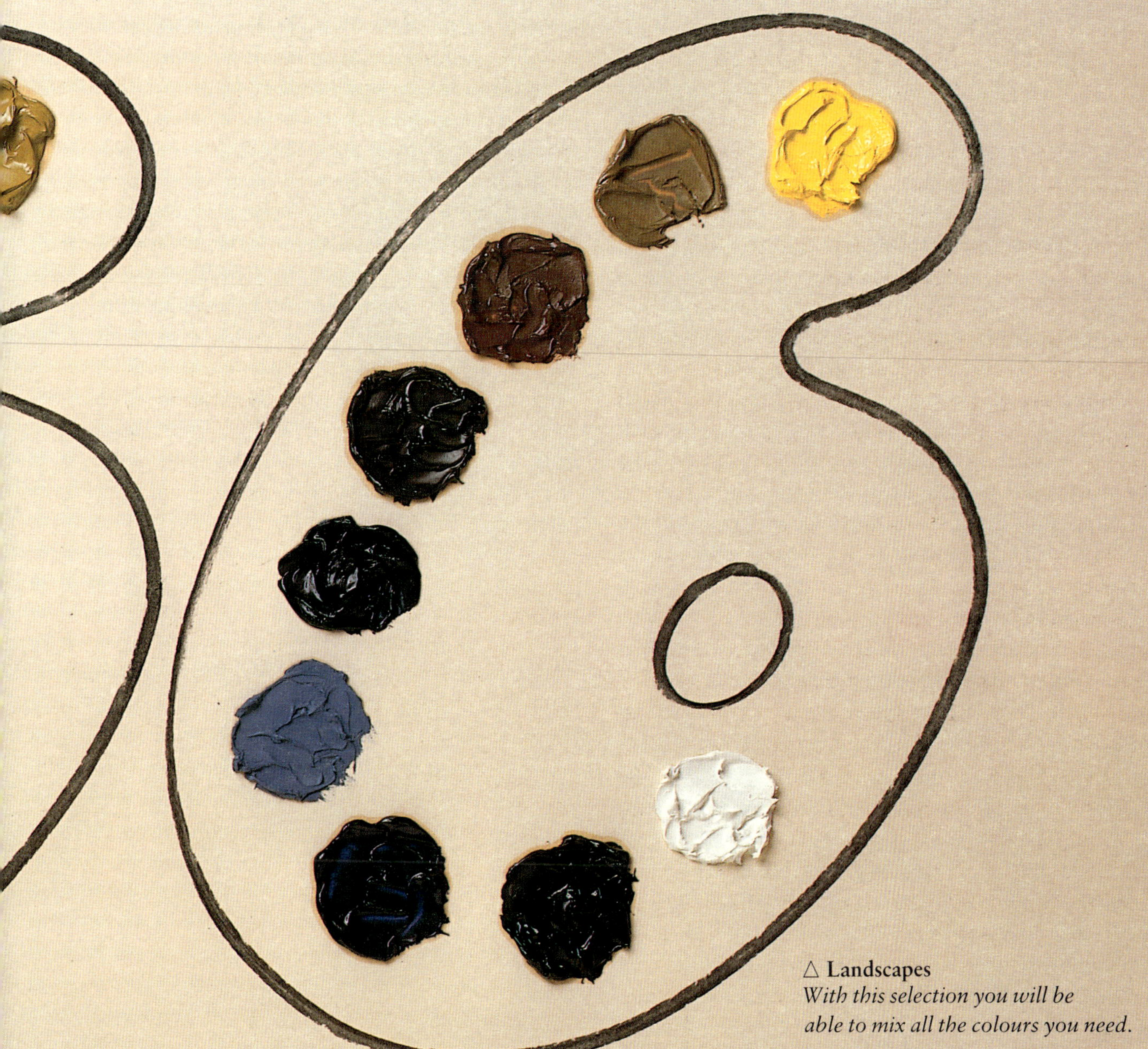

△ **Landscapes**
With this selection you will be able to mix all the colours you need.

A basic palette for flesh tones
For figures or portraits a palette that includes a good selection of earth colours is useful. The following colours will allow you to mix lovely subtle flesh tones:
yellow ochre, raw umber, light red, alizarin crimson, terre verte, cobalt blue, titanium white.

With this selection you will be able to mix a range of delicate colours – light violets, chalky mauves, warm fawns, peachy pinks, drab greens and pale creams. Every artist evolves their own particular palette of colours and in time you'll devise your own, but this will give you a good start.

A basic palette for landscapes
To paint a landscape you will need a surprisingly large range of greens, and the best way of finding these is to mix them for yourself. My recommended palette includes Prussian blue, a cool colour which gives a good range of sharp greens, and ultramarine, which is a warm blue producing muddier greens. This is a good working palette for landscape:
cadmium yellow light, raw sienna, burnt sienna, burnt umber, Prussian blue, cerulean blue, ultramarine blue, black, titanium white.

Viridian is a useful addition. It is rather strong and transparent on its own, but can be mixed with other colours to produce a range of greens.

USING PAINT

Before you start, make sure you have all the equipment you need: tubes of paint, a palette or something to mix paint on, a brush, some turpentine in a pot and one, or two, pots of white spirit for cleaning your brush. You will also need some rags.

Squeeze a little of each colour on to your palette. Lay the colours out around the edge, leaving the centre of the palette free for mixing. Most painters develop a consistent method of laying out colours so that a particular colour is easy to find. There are many systems. A popular method is to lay out the warm colours first, starting with the palest, such as yellow, and working through oranges and reds to the greens and blues on the cool side of the spectrum. White and black can be placed together at one end, or they can be placed at opposite ends. Earth colours are sometimes grouped together, either on one side or with the reds and yellows.

Putting out all your colours before you start has advantages, especially if you intend to work quickly and finish the painting in one sitting – a method known as painting *alla prima*. If all your colours are on the palette, you can concentrate on painting, and not waste time searching for tubes of paint. Another system is to start with a limited palette of two or three colours plus white and see what colours the subject and the painting suggest to you, that is, to let the painting evolve its own colour key.

Start by dipping your brush in the turpentine, then pull some colour from the blob of paint on the palette and blend the paint and turpentine together in the centre of the palette. To mix a new colour, pick up a bit of the second colour and mix that with the first. Add more of each until you get the colour you want. Load your brush with the colour and apply it to the support.

If you will need a lot of a mixed colour, use a painting knife to pick up paint from the edge of the palette, then use the flat of the knife to mix the paints together. When the paint is mixed, you can use a brush dipped in turpentine to dilute it to the right consistency.

Because oil is such an exciting and seductive medium, the beginner often gets carried away and uses too many colours, mixing them in an uncontrolled way. The palette gets messy and the colours on the canvas become muddy; the painter is disappointed with the result and, what is worse, doesn't learn from the process. Even if you are naturally flamboyant, try to curb your enthusiasm to start with. Keep your palette clean and orderly and don't mix more than two colours together in addition to white. Wipe your brush on a rag and wash it in white spirit before you change to a new colour. In this way your colours will stay fresh, and because you know how a particular colour was achieved, you will increase your understanding of paint and colour mixing. As your knowledge and confidence increase, you will evolve a more flexible and personal approach.

◁ *Use the middle of the palette to mix colours. Continue adding colour to the mixture until you get the shade you want. As you can see, you can get a lovely range of subtle colours from this very limited palette.*

◁ *The flesh-tint palette laid out with the warm colours on one side and the cools on the other. From left to right: titanium white, yellow ochre, light red, alizarin crimson, raw umber, terre verte, cobalt blue.*

TECHNIQUES

PAINTING WET-INTO-WET

One of the characteristics of oil paint is that it dries slowly unless you add media which accelerate the drying time. A wet paint surface is alive. It allows you to blend new paint with the existing layer of paint in such a way that it will be impossible for a viewer to tell at what stage a particular colour was added. This means that you can work slowly, leaving your painting for a time, then coming back to it and resuming from where you left off. This has several advantages. It allows you to get to know a subject intimately, to look at it carefully, change your mind, leave it, think about it and then continue working on it at a later date. It is especially useful for people who have only a limited amount of time for painting, as it means you can do a little each day and continue to work into a wet surface. The rate at which oil paint dries depends on the type of ground you use. Gesso (a traditional chalk and size ground), for example, is absorbent and the paint will dry more quickly here than on an acrylic primer. Drying time is also affected by the amount of diluent you have added to the paint and the thickness of the paint layer. Paint thinned with turpentine will dry more quickly than paint used direct from the tube.

Blending colours

Another quality of oil paint is the way that it holds the brush or the knife, and many techniques exploit this to create textural effects. Working wet-into-wet, it is also possible to blend colours so as to achieve smooth, unmodulated surfaces in which the mark of the brush is almost entirely obliterated. Some painters use this approach over the entire surface of a painting; others use it in parts, contrasting areas of rich texture with smoothly blended passages.

Fat over lean

'Fat' describes paint rich in oil. Some colours are naturally fatty, but paint can be made fat by adding an oil such as linseed oil. 'Lean' paint contains little oil or is thinned with a diluent such as turpentine. Because lean paint dries more quickly than fat paint, and contracts less, you should always paint 'fat over lean' to ensure that the paint layer remains stable as it dries. Start by mixing your paint with a little turpentine, but as the layers build up, add more oil and less turpentine.

Oiling out

If parts of a painting become dull as it dries, you can give it a sheen by rubbing a little linseed oil into the dull area. Oiling out a painting by moistening the entire surface is also useful if you decide to rework a painting after it has dried. A slightly oily surface takes the paint better and is pleasanter to work on than a dry surface.

Blending *By working into wet paint it is possible to achieve very gradual transitions between one colour and another, or one tone and another. Practise doing this on a piece of scrap paper.*

◁ **Wet-into-wet** *This painting was done with a brush. The artist continued to work into the wet surface until it was complete. In some areas the paint is fairly flat and unmodulated (the checked cloth, for example) and in others you can still see the mark of the brush, but texture is not a particularly important element of the painting. Compare this with the pictures on pages 62 and 64, in which the artist has deliberately built up a thick paint layer.*

TECHNIQUES

WAYS OF MIXING COLOURS

There are several ways of mixing colour in oil paint. The most obvious is by combining two or more pigments on the palette, or sometimes on the canvas. Learning to mix colours is a demanding but exciting business. You can read books on the subject but only by patient experiment will you learn which colour mixtures produce the colours you want. So spend time getting to know the colours you use and what you can do with them. Mix colours in different proportions and put dabs of the mixed colour on a scrap of paper to see if they are exactly what you want. In time you will hold these colour 'recipes' in your head, but you will never exhaust the possibilities of your palette.

Because oil stays wet for so long you can change colours on the canvas by mixing another colour into the wet paint. Be careful, though, not to overwork the paint – if you mix too many colours the paint becomes dull. Oil paint looks best when it is fresh. With experience you will be able to judge just how far you can go.

Optical colour mixing

This is the term used to describe the blending of colours which occurs in the eye rather than on the canvas or palette. The system, sometimes known as Pointillism or Divisionism, was devised in the late nineteenth century by the French painters Signac and Seurat after a careful study of optics and colour theory. These artists used the system in a very formal way, as you can see if you study their paintings in galleries or books. If you put dashes and dots of different colours on a canvas, you will find that the separate colours do indeed begin to merge as you move away from the canvas, creating new colours. So an area painted with dabs of yellow and red appears orange, while blue and yellow dabs placed side by side will appear green. Colours mixed in this way are often more intense than those mixed on the palette because the paints are in their purest form, and are not affected by the interaction of pigments and the media used in the paint.

A less rigid system of optical colour mixing is called broken colour. This effect is achieved in several ways: by laying touches of different un-

△ Red and yellow being mixed on the palette.

blended colours side by side, or by applying one layer of colour over another so that the underlying colour shows through. By dipping the tip of your brush into first one colour and then another and by applying the loaded brush to the canvas, you can create a striated brushstroke which contains mixed, partially mixed and unmixed colour, making for a lively paint surface. This partial mixing of colour sometimes happens by mistake and in time you will learn how to exploit these 'accidental' colour effects.

△ *An orange mixed from the red and yellow.*

△ *The partially mixed, broken colour effect achieved when the same red and yellow paint are picked up on the brush and worked on to the canvas.*

△ *Dots of red and yellow paint placed side by side. Seen from a distance these merge in the eye to create a vibrant orange.*

Scumbling

In this technique a thin layer of opaque or semi-opaque paint is loosely brushed over a ground or a previously applied colour in such a way that the first colour shows through in places and modifies the scumbled colour. The paint may be scrubbed on with a stiff brush, or rubbed on with fingertips or a cloth. This technique is a useful way of laying in an underpainting which is not too dominant or of 'knocking back' an area of colour that has become too dominant. You could, for example, scumble dark green over a green which was too garish. It can also be used to create special effects like clouds or mists on the horizon.

Drybrushing

In drybrushing the brush has very little paint on it, so that when it is dragged across a surface, especially a coarse-grained canvas, it leaves a trail of mottled colour. To achieve a drybrush effect load a stiff-bristled brush with colour and then blot it on cloth or paper so that it is almost dry. The effect is enhanced if you spread the bristles of the brush so that they are separate, then drag the brush across the surface at a shallow angle so that the flat of the brush rather than the tip touches the support. This technique is useful for creating special effects like grass, fur or feathers.

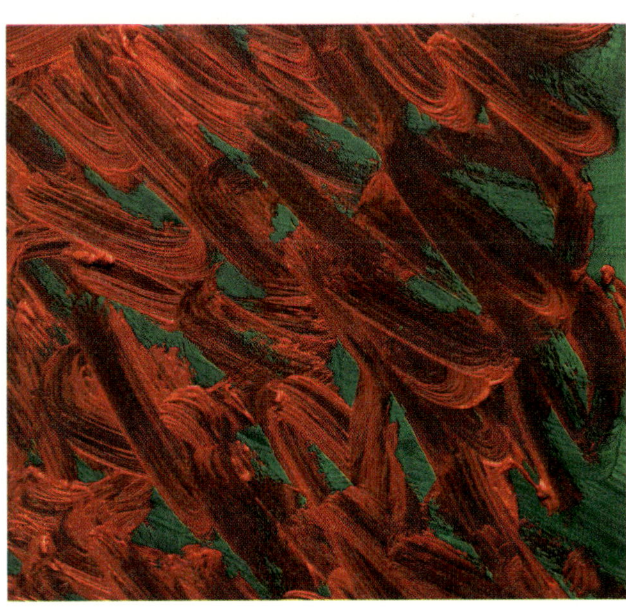

▷ *Red scumbled loosely over green. In places the underlying green shows through and modifies the red; in other bits of pure green remain, creating complex and shimmering colour.*

△ *This image has been created using flat, untextured colour.*

▽ *Creamy paint is then scumbled on to create an uneven covering which suggests clouds.*

▽ *Similarly, the dense foliage of the tree is broken up by scumbling on a lighter green.*

TECHNIQUES

GLAZING

In oil painting a glaze describes a transparent film of colour which allows you to modify an area of colour without obliterating it. A glaze can be applied over a tinted ground, an underpainting, an area of impasto or even another glaze. Traditional oil paintings were developed in two stages: a monochrome underpainting, followed by carefully controlled layers of colour applied as glazes and scumbles (opaque and semi-opaque layers of colour). The resulting paintings had a special luminosity and depth, often described as an 'inner light'. This can be seen in the works of masters such as Jan van Eyck (*c.* 1395–1441) and Rembrandt (1606–69).

It is possible to produce an entire painting by building up layers of glazes, but these days it is more usual to combine glazing with direct painting. The best way of understanding the possibilities of glazing is to make a small painting using a glazing technique. Start with a monochrome underpainting and allow that to dry completely before you start to glaze. If you do the underpainting in oil, the drying time could be several days, but you can speed things up by using acrylic paint, which will dry in hours.

To make a glaze, mix the paint with linseed oil and a little turpentine. Or use one of the alkyd-based oil media, which are excellent for glazing and dry more quickly than traditional oil media. You can glaze the whole painting with a single colour, or use different colours in adjacent areas. Allow one layer of colour to dry before you apply the next and, remembering the fat-over-lean rule, add more medium to each layer of glaze.

Glazes can be used to create shadow areas of great luminosity and depth, and they can be brushed over highlights to give them added brilliance. Glazing is particularly useful in areas such as figure painting or portraiture in which you need to achieve subtle modifications and transitions of colour and tone in order to render the delicate tones of flesh. You can use a glaze to give unity to a painting or parts of a painting. For example, if the modelling of a portrait looks too crude, a glaze may pull the tones together.

△ *Ultramarine is mixed with Wingel, an alkyd medium, to create a transparent glaze. You could also use linseed oil with turpentine.*

▷ *A glaze of ultramarine is laid over cadmium yellow pale. Notice the way the yellow shines through the transparent blue layer.*

IMPASTO TECHNIQUES

Applied thickly, oil paint can be used to build up a luscious and richly textured surface in which the marks of brush, knife or even fingers play an important part. The term impasto is used to describe this low-relief surface and the technique of applying paint in this way. With impasto the way the paint is applied, and the tool with which it is applied, become yet another means of artistic expression. The viewer can enjoy the almost three-dimensional quality of the paint surface and get a sense of the excitement with which the artist handled the paint.

Until the end of the nineteenth century, impasto techniques were generally combined with layered and blended paint effects. Rembrandt, for example, combined overlapping layers of semi-transparent scumbles and transparent glazes with passages of richly textured paint. Sometimes swathes of paint were applied wet-into-wet, the fluid brushstrokes modelling forms such as hands or the folds of drapery. At other times encrustations of paint were used to capture the texture of crisply pleated collars, lace or intricately worked jewellery. Impasto was often used for highlights, the opaque colour contrasting with the transparent layers of colour used to give depth to shadows. Often his impastos were also glazed.

For the artist Vincent Van Gogh (1853–1890), impasto was a principal means of expression, used over the entire picture surface rather than confined to specific areas. He worked directly with a brush or knife loaded with paint, sometimes using his fingers to move the paint about, mixing colour on the canvas rather than on the palette, and even applying it directly from the tube. His brushstrokes emphasize form and imply energy. There are swirling lines, short stabbing strokes, staccato lines and lines which undulate across the picture surface.

△ **Impasto with a brush** *In this painting the mark of the brush gives the painting a lively surface. Notice the way the direction of the brushstrokes follows and describes the form of the lemon. Compare this with the treatments of the same subject on pages 56 and 64.*

▽ **Glazing over impasto** *Glazes can be applied over heavily textured passages. Here the separate areas of textured colour are clearly visible.*

Creating texture with the brush

To exploit the textural qualities of oil paint to the full you will need to work boldly and broadly. This can be difficult when you are unfamiliar with the medium and therefore inclined to be tentative. Start by making a painting of a simple still-life subject. Use a small support 12 in × 16 in (30 cm × 40 cm) and a brush which is slightly larger than you would normally choose (a number 8 bristle, say). Mix only a little turps with the paint.

△ *A glaze of transparent colour is washed over the lemon.*

△ *The glaze modifies the underlying colour without obliterating it.*

▷ **The marks of the brush** *Every brush can be used to create a range of different marks, depending on whether you use the tip or the side, how much pressure you apply and the sort of gesture you use. Here we show a range of marks made with a round and a flat bristle brush. On a piece of paper experiment to see how many different marks you can get from a single brush. Explore the possibilities of different kinds of brushes.*

Painting with a knife

Although a brush is the normal implement used for applying paint to a support, you can use anything you like. What you use will depend on the effect you are trying to achieve, the area you have to cover, the speed at which you want to work, the tools you have to hand – in fact, what you feel like using. In the first project on page *71*, for example, the artist uses a rag to apply the underpainting. He did this in order to get the canvas covered as quickly as possible and to simplify the image. Although the brush has undoubtedly proved itself the most popular and versatile painting tool over hundreds of years, you should, nevertheless, explore different ways of applying paint from time to time. It will keep your work fresh.

The painting knife is a convenient and flexible painting tool. It can be used to add texture to parts of a painting – to scratch back into the paint surface or to create areas of crisp impasto. It is also possible to do an entire painting with the knife. This is a particularly useful technique for paintings done *alla prima* (in one sitting) as the knife allows you to trowel on the paint so that the colour builds up fast. Painting knives are available in a variety of shapes and sizes and can be used to make a range of marks. The paint should be rich and thick if it is to hold the mark of the knife. You can dab on separate patches of pure colour, or use the tip to flick in shapes and the flat of the knife to slur colours together to create a relatively smooth paint surface.

△ The crisp surface of this painting has been achieved using a knife. Compare the detail above with the detail of the picture on page 71 which was painted with a brush.

These marks are made with a palette knife. Experiment for yourself!

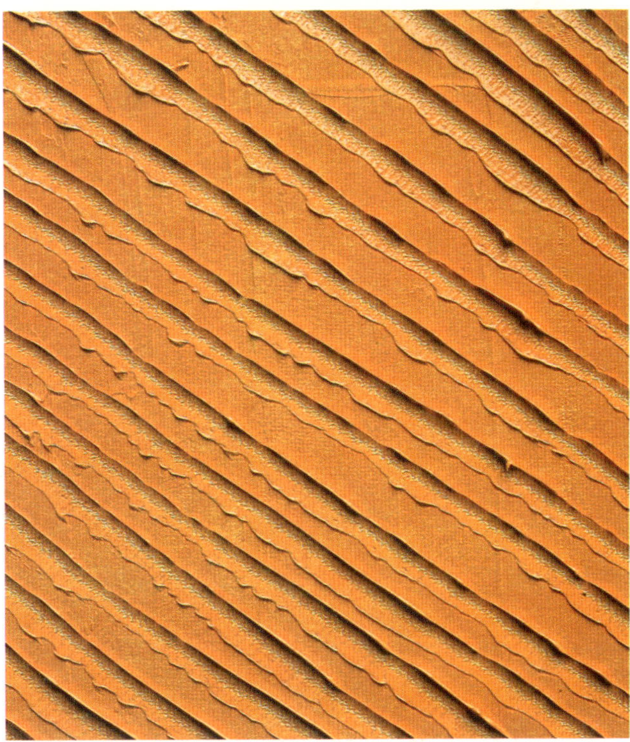

TECHNIQUES

STARTING A PAINTING

Making the first mark on that brilliant white canvas is probably the most difficult thing the artist, especially the beginner, has to do. Here are several different ways of starting a painting.

Underdrawing in charcoal

An underdrawing may be made directly on to a white ground, or on to a ground that has been tinted with a colour. It can be made in almost any medium, including charcoal, pencil and even paint. Charcoal is often used for underdrawing because it has a pleasingly fluid line, can be used on almost any surface, is easily amended or erased and is unlikely to damage the support. It is especially useful if you have to make a lot of changes, perhaps because you lack confidence about your drawing skills, or are unsure about how to organize the composition. The underdrawing is not a detailed study of the subject – that sort of exploratory drawing should be made in a sketchbook as a separate exercise. The underdrawing merely allows

Underdrawing in charcoal

◁ 1 *Using a thin stick of willow charcoal, draw in the main outlines of the subject. Concentrate on the broad shapes and the way they fill the rectangle. Work quickly and directly and don't worry if you have to redraw lines several times; it doesn't matter what the drawing looks like.*

△ 2 *The underdrawing helps you organize the image on the picture area. It is not a detailed study of the subject.*

you to establish the broad areas of the painting and to indicate where they will fall in relation to the edges of the support and to each other.

Using a thin or medium stick of willow charcoal, make an outline drawing of the subject. Use a soft, clean cloth to erase incorrect lines or to remove the whole drawing so that you can start again if necessary.

Because charcoal dust would discolour the paint, you must either fix the finished underdrawing with a spray fixative or 'knock it back' by flicking it with a cloth. Knocking back removes loose particles of charcoal while retaining a faint outline of the drawing which is an adequate guide for the first stages of the painting. Some artists reinforce the charcoal outline by going over it in thinned paint.

△ 3 *When you are satisfied with the composition, remove the charcoal by flicking it with a duster, or by brushing it lightly with a soft brush. The remaining pale outline will be sufficient to guide you when you start to paint.*

Tinting a ground

A white ground is very stark and even a bit frightening, so many artists start by applying a layer of transparent colour to the ground. This was a usual method of working from the seventeenth century until the late nineteenth century, when the Impressionists started to paint on white grounds. You will probably find a tinted ground easier to work on at the beginning. Choose a middle tone, because it will give you a base on which to apply lighter tones and highlights, as well as mid- to dark tones. You will be able to work up to the lights and down to the darks. You will find that the tinted ground provides a key against which to judge the other tones and also holds the whole painting together. A painting done in this way begins really to look like something very early on. You can either tint a ground before you do the underdrawing or wash a tint on over it. Allow the tint to dry completely before beginning to paint over it. Acrylic paint is an especially useful medium for tinting because it dries so quickly.

▷ 1 *Choose a mid-tone which is neutral or relates to the subject you are painting. For example, a muted green would be helpful for a landscape painting, while blue would be an obvious choice for a seascape. Here the artist has used raw umber. Mix the colour with plenty of turpentine and apply it to the surface with a large brush. Cover the entire surface working briskly. If you want a very pale tint, leave it for a few minutes and then wipe it off with a clean cloth. If you are tinting a large area, use a cloth, sponge or paper to apply the colour; it will be quicker.*

Underpainting

You can start a painting with a brush drawing in thinned paint. This is a very direct method of working and allows you to lay in a drawing quickly. It is particularly useful if you work on a large scale, as you can suit the size of the brush to the scale of the painting. On a large painting charcoal lines would look frail and tentative, whereas a big brush will allow you to work fast with bold, vigorous lines.

A brush painting is ideal if you are working *alla prima*, out of doors. First, it is simple and means you have one less piece of equipment to take. Second, because you are using paint and brush rather than charcoal, the drawing feels more immediate and this means you can start the painting with the directness and energy appropriate to *alla prima* work.

If you are new to painting and drawing, rather than merely to oil painting, it is worth reiterating that you should choose a brush slightly larger than you think you will need. Beginners often draw hesitantly and are distracted by unimportant details. A big brush will counteract that tendency and encourage you to be bold and direct, to concentrate on the broad aspects of the composition rather than fiddly details.

A brush drawing can also be used to reinforce the faint trace of a charcoal drawing, so that you can see the drawing during the early stages of the painting.

Use a neutral colour such as grey or brown, or a colour which is suggested by the subject – green for a landscape or blue for a seascape, for example. Blue is used for underpainting because it is a clean colour and recedes. Paul Cézanne (1839–1906) often used a blue underdrawing, and because he frequently worked very thinly and didn't cover the entire canvas with paint, the blue lines of the underdrawing are evident in the final painting.

Monochrome underpainting

A traditional method of starting a painting is to do an underpainting in tones of a single colour on a white ground. This allows you to establish the broad forms of the subject and the tonal values without taking any decisions about colour. Choose a neutral colour or a colour appropriate to the subject and thin the paint with turpentine. You can either do an outline drawing and then block in the mid- and dark tones, leaving the white of the canvas to stand for highlights, or you can block in areas of tone without drawing first. The approach you adopt will depend on your skill, confidence and personality. Some people like things sorted out in an orderly fashion – drawing first, then tones, then colour – while others like to avoid committing themselves too early. To 'see' the tones in a subject, half close your eyes and look for the middle tones. Then look for the darkest and the lightest areas. It helps if you let your eye travel over the subject, comparing one area with another. In that way you can decide which parts are equivalent in tone, and where the maximum contrasts are.

Brush drawing

▷ **1** *Choose a neutral colour or a colour which relates to the subject. Here the artist has used black. Thin the paint with turpentine and, using a small bristle or hair brush, start to draw in the outlines of the subject. Study the subject and think about the way it will fit the picture area. Do not be afraid to redraw lines several times; if the drawing gets too messy, you can wipe them off with a cloth. The most common mistake is making the subject of the painting too small in relation to the picture area, so be bold.*

△ 2 *The finished drawing should be a simple outline with perhaps an indication of the darkest tones. The intention is to sort out the composition, not to make a detailed drawing.*

△ 2 *The rim and part of the middle of the plate were lighter than any other area. The darkest areas were under the plate and between the apples.*

Monochrome underpainting

△ 1 *Using thinned paint in a mid-tone, block in all the parts of the painting that appear to you to be neither light nor dark. Leave the white of the canvas to stand for the lightest areas.*

△ 3 *Once the broad forms have been established and the distribution of lights and darks has been roughly established, you can assess the composition and make adjustments as necessary.*

PROJECTS

STILL LIFE WITH ARTICHOKE FLOWER

In this project I have done everything I can to make it easy for you to begin your first oil painting. A stark white canvas can be daunting, so the artist has toned the ground. The still-life group has been assembled from everyday household objects and the artist, Stan Smith, has used a rag to block in the underpainting, a specially direct method of painting intended to overcome any hesitancy on your part and to get you started.

△ *In this still-life group simple shapes, warm, neutral colours and natural textures are set against the cool white tones and crisp texture of the tablecloth. A length of linen canvas was used as a backdrop, the oatmeal colour picking up the predominant colour theme and pulling the group together.*

Setting up the still-life group

Still life is a marvellous subject for the painter: the possibilities are limitless and the materials are always near to hand – you can select them, move them about and light them as you wish. Any group of objects, no matter how apparently random, will trigger ideas if you study it carefully.

In this still-life group the most obvious themes are colour, texture and shape. It is not a 'colourful' arrangement, but it is nevertheless full of wonderfully subtle warm ochres and muted greys, which contrast with the cool whites and blues of the table-cloth. The natural textures of the stoneware pot and wooden spoons, the basket and the oyster mushrooms, and the dried head of the artichoke are set off by the crispness of the table-cloth. The tall spoons give the arrangement a strong vertical emphasis, but the dominant shapes are the ellipses of the pot and the basket and the repeated ovals of the spoons, which contrast with the angularity of the blue border and the folds of the fabric. Notice also the way the objects can be seen as a single shape against the background.

Make a selection of objects that interest you and see if you can find any linking shapes and colours. Ideally something – an unusual shape or colour – will grab your interest and provide a focus for the composition. Put the still life together quickly, then spend time studying it, looking for the compositional possibilities, the 'hooks' for the painting. The idea is to 'make a painting', not merely to 'copy' what is in front of you. Your painting should communicate your response to the subject and express the excitement you felt painting it.

Toning the ground

When choosing a support, you are looking for a size you will feel comfortable with and a shape which suits the subject. Here the artist has used a portrait (vertical) canvas, 30 in × 20 in (76 cm × 51 cm), because the subject is vertical. He has toned the ground with thinned paint in a middle tone. This simplifies the painting process, providing a key for you to work against.

▽ *A stark white canvas can be intimidating. A toned ground makes it easier to start and also simplifies the painting process by providing a middle tone. As you add the lights and darks, the broad forms of the painting emerge very quickly. Here the artist uses raw umber thinned with turpentine. He applies the colour freely, creating a loosely textured surface which will become part of the painting. Allow the canvas to dry before you progress to the next stage. The toning can be done with acrylic paint, which dries quickly.*

△ *Start by making quick sketches of the subject. Move around, looking for the most interesting viewpoint. Try looking down on the group from above, then crouch down and see what it looks like when seen from eye-level. Use a viewfinder – a window cut from card or paper – to help you frame the subject. Work in a sketchbook, using pencil or charcoal.*

◁△ *The artist made two sketches in which he experimented with different compositions. By placing the main elements slightly to the right of centre he created interesting background shapes. Always look for these 'negative shapes', the background spaces between the objects, and between the objects and the four sides of the canvas. It is best to avoid placing the main elements of the picture right in the middle – asymmetry generally works better than symmetry.*

△ *The artist mixes a dark tone and, working very quickly, blocks in the broad shapes of the pot, the basket and the spoons. Now, with white paint thinned with a little turps, he starts to lay in the pale tones of the background. Remember the fat-over-lean rule and mix a little turps with the paint; don't add oil at this stage.*

Preliminary drawings

Make several exploratory sketches at this stage. These will help you decide how much of the subject to include and how to arrange it within the picture frame. Use these drawings to look for rhythms and repeated forms, for angles and directions. The more drawings you do, the more you will see in the subject, and the more possibilities you will find. These drawings should be jotted down quickly, the sketchier the better. It is the looking and the analysing of what you see that are important, not the finished drawing.

Working with a limited palette

It is a good idea to start with a limited range of colours, eight at the most. Here the artist has used titanium white, cobalt blue, viridian, raw umber, alizarin crimson, cadmium red, cadmium yellow and some black. Using a limited selection like this, you can achieve an almost infinite range of colours and tones. A good way of mixing colours is to work with ones from different sides of the colour wheel. For example, if you mix the complementaries red and green, you should in theory produce a pure neutral grey. In fact, because of the impurity of pigments you don't, but you do get the most marvellous warm and cool neutrals. You can make them veer towards the cool side by adding more of the cool colour and more to the warm side by adding more of the warm colour. This is a lovely way to mix colours and particularly suited to a picture with a subtle and limited range of tones.

△ *This system of painting has several advantages. The extreme tonal contrasts of the underpainting provide an excellent basis for subsequent layers in which the tones can be refined. It also allows you to 'see' the main structures of the composition, because the positive shapes of the objects and the negative shapes of the background are quickly established. If the artist had been working with a brush out of a white background, the process would have been much more complicated and the simple yet dynamic arrangements would not have been so obvious.*

Painting with a rag

At first it is difficult to work broadly and simply, the temptation being to focus on the details of a particular area rather than to deal with the whole painting. Even experienced painters find that their

work becomes tight and from time to time experiment with a different approach or a change of medium to free themselves up. A rag is a splendid means of applying paint because it forces you to generalize and to work fast, which means that you really 'get into' the painting quickly.

Using gesture

Choose a long-handled brush and move away from the canvas. This will force you to use bold, fluid elbow and shoulder movements. The more restricted movements, using the wrist as pivot, are best suited to detailed, close work. Gesture is an important and expressive aspect of painting. Study the work of Van Gogh and you will find swirling, sweeping swathes of paint, and tiny, agitated brushmarks, each creating a different kind of energy and texture.

Reviewing progress

The painting was allowed to dry for a day because a wet surface is slippery and difficult to work. Leaving the painting for a while also means that when you return, you can assess it with a fresh eye.

▽ Though simply rendered and generalized, the painting is already convincingly established. The areas of colour relate to each other because of the underlying tonal painting and there is a sense of dimension and structure even though there are no linear elements. The paint surface has a pleasing tactile quality, which is one of the pleasures of oil paint.

△ The artist starts to block in local colour (the actual colour of the object) and accidental colour (colour reflected from surrounding objects). These are the colours that he actually sees rather than the colours he knows to be there. For the aubergine he uses a blackish-purply mix, with a bit of blue and lighter purple, and a touch of pink on top. This will provide a guide for the next stage. The peppers are put in with a bright mixed green, while a warm mixed grey is used for the mushrooms.

Study it from a distance, considering it as a whole, then looking at colour, tone and composition in turn. Half closing your eyes will help you concentrate and will exaggerate the tonal contrasts – which is why artists are so often seen squinting at their paintings.

Having established the broad outlines of the painting and put in the local colour in a positive way, the next stage is to cover the ground and develop subtle contrasts from the rather abrupt ones created so far. Imagine the painting as a series of pictures, each more sharply focused than the ones before. At every stage the painting becomes more accurate and more subtle.

Enjoying paint

Oil is an infinitely flexible medium, capable of capturing the qualities of any surface or texture. It can be used thickly, thinly, blended or as dabs of pure impasto, in layers or applied directly to the canvas. It is also a marvellously sensuous medium, and you should not be afraid to enjoy its tactile qualities – thick, creamy impastos of pure pigment that can be sculpted with the knife or brush; clear, brilliant glazes that stain the ground; or delicate scumbles of thin colour which trickle down the canvas. Young children have this delight in paint, but most of us lose it as we grow older. We become rather prim and favour a smooth, carefully modelled, rather impersonal surface. Try and recapture that childlike delight in paint for its own sake. It will make you sensitive to the quality of the paint surface and will enrich and enliven your work.

Mixing colour

Mixing colour is difficult, especially when you are working within quite a limited range – as on the basket, for example. Study an area carefully, analyse the colour you see and mix an equivalent on the palette. Put that on to the canvas but be

◁ *At this stage the artist changes to brush and knife in order to develop the detail within the painting. The knife was used to give the drapery a crisp, angular feel. Be sensitive to the quality of materials. A thin cotton fabric should look crisp and thin, not heavy like a blanket. Look for ways of expressing the hardness of the glazed surface of the pot, the flaccidity of the mushrooms, and the brittleness of the artichoke.*

prepared to make adjustments. Because colour is affected by adjacent colour, what looks right on the palette may look very different on the canvas.

A useful way of identifying colour and tone is to allow your eye to travel over the subject, making comparisons and finding equivalents – for example, the highlight on the jar is the brightest part of the jar, but it is not as bright as the brightest part of the tablecloth. And although the pot is predominantly warm in tone, it picks up cool reflections from the white cloth.

◁ The artist has put down a band of colour with a knife and now tonks, or blots, it with paper. This leaves a positive shape on the canvas, but because there is very little paint on the surface he can paint over it immediately.

▷ With a number 5 bristle brush and creamy paint the artist develops the whole picture surface, putting down paint and then standing back to judge the effect. His eye travels backwards and forwards between subject and canvas, and across the subject and the canvas, comparing and contrasting tones and colours.

◁ A light middle tone was used as the base for the basket. Into this the artist puts dark touches with a soft brush, to indicate the texture of the rings of raffia.

Adding texture

Oil paint can be built up in layers and thick impastos to create a textured surface which holds the mark of the brush, knife or even fingers. You can also scratch back into the wet paint with a knife, the end of the brush or a pencil – this technique is called sgrafitto. You can even mix media. Here, for example, the artist used a variety of techniques to create a visually exciting and descriptive paint surface. On this page you can see him using waxy pencil on the dry paint to create crisp edges, to suggest the woven surface of the basket and to add interest to the picture surface. He uses blue pastel to define the patterned border of the white cloth.

△ If you look at the basket again, you'll see that it has been rendered in several different ways. There is dark on a middle tone, light on a middle tone and in the foreground, where it catches the light, there is light on dark. Look carefully and paint what you see.

As the painting progresses the forms emerge more convincingly, and the objects settle into their place in space. Underlying layers of paint, even the ground, show through in parts, informing and modifying subsequent layers. The muted background, for example, is warmed by the raw umber which was used to tone the ground.

△ A pencil is used to scratch a criss-cross texture on the edge of the basket. Elsewhere it is used to draw into the wet paint.

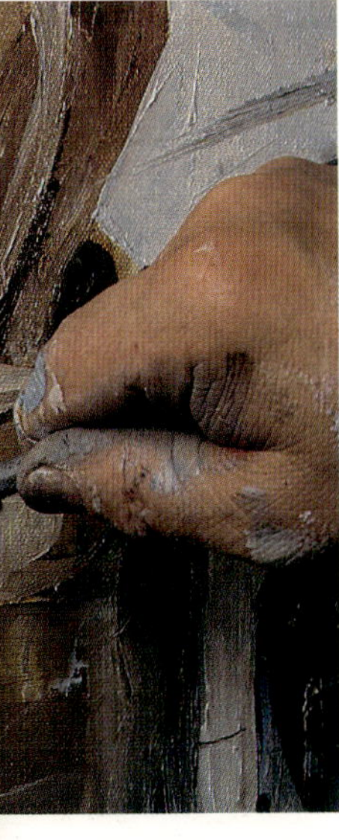

◁ *Texture is graffitoed into the surface of the pot with a pencil.*

▽ *Oil pastel is used to add texture and detail to the decorative border.*

▷ *The artist continues to work into the painting, never concentrating on one area but always seeing the painting as a whole. He scumbles a cool green over the background, which gives this area more solidity while at the same time pushing it back in space, so that it definitely sits behind the still-life group. The finished painting works on several levels. It is a realistic representation of the collection of objects. However, the artist has not copied slavishly but has made the subject his own by a process of selection and editing, and by his choice of colour and the lively treatment of the paint surface. I hope you too will produce something which is uniquely your own.*

Finishing a painting

When is a painting finished? That's a difficult question to answer. It's finished when you think it's finished – although, having decided that a painting is finished, six months later you might take it out and work on it again. Some artists keep paintings around them in the studio, glancing at them as they work on other canvases. One day they suddenly realize that a single touch will pull the whole thing together. Others work on a single canvas spasmodically for years. Beginners sometimes overwork a painting, so that the paint surface becomes muddy and loses its freshness and spontaneity. Try living with your painting for a few days before you add the final flourishes.

PROJECTS

GARDEN FLOWERS AGAINST A RED BACKGROUND

For our second project we have chosen a challenging subject and a very different approach. Flowers are a lovely subject for the painter, with their wonderful bright, paintbox colours and the infinitely varied shapes of petals, leaves and flowerheads. Each flower has a special quality. Think, for example, of the ruched and overblown frilliness of old-fashioned roses, the bobbing bonnets of aquilegia and the stark geometry of irises. But this obvious beauty can be an impediment to good painting, for the painter may feel it necessary to produce a 'pretty' painting. Flower paintings are just another form of still life and should be painted with the same rigour and robustness.

Red against red

Our bunch of garden flowers includes roses and peonies in assorted reds, pinks and whites. To make the project more exciting – and challenging – we've set them against a vivid red backdrop, creating a symphony of dry pinks, blue pinks and a demanding combination of reds. These will have to be mixed on the palette and made to work on the canvas. The spatial arrangements within the painting present another problem. In Chapter 4 I talked about the way warm colours appear to advance and cool colours appear to recede. Here is a 'hot' background which will have to be handled carefully if it is not to advance and overwhelm the flower group.

◁ *Think carefully about the way you will crop the image; a paper or card viewfinder is useful.*

▷ *Ultramarine blue thinned with turpentine is used for the underdrawing. The artist wants to get a sense of the flowers spraying from the pot. He is also looking for strong diagonals to balance the diagonal of the table edge. He avoids placing the pot in the centre and also makes sure that radiating diagonals aren't totally regular – unconscious symmetry in a painting can be jarring.*

△ *The subject is exciting and colourful – warm reds and pinks sparkle against their complementary greens, while the cool grey of the pot and the whites of the flowers and the tablecloth act as a counterpoint.*

◁ *The mass of green foliage is blocked in using thin, transparent paint. The artist works quickly, looking for the broad areas of colour rather than details. You should use a long-handled brush and step back from the canvas to squint at the subject. A darker tone is then used to block in darker areas.*

Composing the group

When the group was first set up, the horizontal of the line between the red background and the white tablecloth in the foreground created a rather static image. By shifting the angle of the table, the artist, Stan Smith, introduced a strong diagonal stress which is more interesting and dynamic, and balances the strong vertical of the pot.

Linear underpainting

To capture the fresh brilliance of the colours, the artist selects a white, primed canvas and does the underdrawing in paint, because charcoal would dirty the surface. He chooses blue, which is a clean, recessive colour often used for underpaintings.

The artist uses the underdrawing to position the object within the rectangle of the picture area and to explore the compositional possibilities. The first marks are about rhythm and structure rather than about individual details and proportions. He finds a strong diagonal running top left to bottom right, and interestingly, this counterbalances the diagonal of the tablecloth. He is careful to place the pot slightly left of centre to avoid absolute symmetry. In this way the artist gives the composition a solid, geometric underpinning, which acts as a counterweight to the organic, rather fluid forms of flowers, leaves and stems. As a result the composition has a satisfying structure and solidity.

△ The reds are blocked in with thin red paint. The artist uses a variety of reds – a yellowish scarlet for the peony on the left and crimson for the roses. The intention is to establish the distribution of the reds providing a guide for later stages.

▷ For the background the artist uses matt red paint applied in a flat, unmodulated way. The background is used to draw back into the bunch of flowers, creating crisp edges. You can see the way the negative shapes of leaves and the white rose have been left. The rose will be glazed at a later stage.

▷ The broad forms of the composition are apparent at this stage. As the paint layer is thin, the artist has a good template for the painting while not being too committed – it is still easy to make adjustments. Be prepared to make changes if a composition is not working. One of the advantages of oil paint is that you can scrub off thin paint with a turpsy rag; even thick impastos can be scraped off with a palette knife.

Set up a similar subject and analyse it in the same way. Use thinned paint, and don't worry if it dribbles down the canvas – you can wipe it off with a rag. Spend some time on the underdrawing, exploring the composition and looking for rhythms, angles and verticals. Don't neglect the four edges of the picture area, for these are an important part of the composition. Think about how you will position the subject in relation to the edges. Use a view-finder cut from paper or card to see what happens if you allow the subject to be cropped on one side, or on all four sides. The impact in each case will be very different.

Blocking in colour

The artist works with a limited palette of cobalt blue, viridian green, sap green, alizarin crimson, cadmium red, cadmium yellow and titanium white.

The background colour is red – the most aggressive and advancing of all colours. If it were introduced too early, it would dominate the canvas and 'throw' all the colour relationships. To avoid this the artist starts by blocking in the mass of green foliage. He mixes a transparent green from viridian and sap green with touches of alizarin crimson – a mid-green that is neither a blue green nor a yellow green. At this stage he is not trying to get the exact colour, but is more interested in locating the green mass and seeing how it works within the composi-

◁ *The anchovy jar is given a blue ground, which will be painted later to give it its special character. This is easier and cleaner than trying to mix a grey at this stage. A blue grey would normally be a cool colour, but the front of the jar looks warm against the white of the cloth. It is by making these comparisons and adjustments that you finally arrive at accurate and convincing interpretations of colour and tone.*

tion. He used a second, darker green tone to create a sense of depth within the foliage. Already the eye begins to travel in and out of the canvas as well as across it.

And remember, at this stage you are investigating, exploring and preparing a base for the next stage. Don't worry about what the finished painting will look like; that will emerge as the work proceeds.

Adding reds

Next the artist starts to block in the pinks and reds of the flowers. Once again he is interested in the distribution of the areas of colour rather than in the exact colours. He uses paint thinned with a little turpentine. The red peony on the left is the only flower that is on the yellow-red side of the spectrum, so he blocks in that with scarlet – cadmium red. The roses are a bluer red, so he mixes

△ *The artist had to find a way of describing the tiny flowers of the cotoneaster. He scooped up thick white paint on the tip of the palette knife and touched it to the canvas so that bits of paint were left behind in a random way. The stickiness of the undiluted paint means that it forms little peaks as the knife pulls away. In other areas, painted with a less loaded knife, the patches of white are more amorphous.*

a crimson and scumbles that on in those areas. He adds a little linseed oil to the crimson mix, creating a transparent glaze which he uses as a base for the pink peony. At this stage he is generalizing the colours and trying to get the overall character of the piece.

More red

The background is blocked in with flat, matt colour with no warming, cooling or tonal variation. The aim is to create as neutral a red as possible, so that the colour is there but sits back and doesn't distract the eye. The background colour can be used to define the silhouette and details such as leaves. The artist has left an area of white canvas to stand for the white flower. Rather than using a thick white impasto he will glaze this area at a later stage to create a delicate and luminous white.

Looking at shadows

A suggestion of the warm shadows on the left of the pot are scumbled in. They will help to establish the flat surface of the table but are also an important compositional element, forming a diagonal with the stem of the white rose. These generalized shadows contrast with the rather staccato movements of those on the right.

Developing the forms

If you try to sort the bunch of flowers leaf by leaf and flower by flower, you'll get in a muddle, and the result will be bitty and unconvincing. Try instead to see a single form comprised of lights and darks,

The painting knife is a splendid tool which can be used to trowel on thick colour and make an almost infinite variety of marks. Here it is used to draw the veins of a leaf by scratching back into the wet paint surface.

◁ More than any other medium, oil paint responds to and reflects the tools with which it is applied. Each tool has an entirely different character which can be used to define shapes and forms. So, a painting knife can be used for crisp edges and tracts of opaque paint. Paint applied with the fingers can be laid on in swirling, gestural passages, or it can be rubbed into the canvas to create areas of softly diffused colour.

with touches of local and reflected colour. Concentrate really hard on the subject, see it as a series of abstract forms and put down exactly what you see. From time to time stand back to assess what you have done. You'll be surprised to find that the patches of colour and tone read as a mass of foliage and flowers.

Adding texture

Oil paint has marvellous textural qualities which can be harnessed to describe different kinds of surfaces within the subject. However, a good painting can be enjoyed on many levels and a rich and varied paint surface can be immensely satisfying.

Study the details on this page carefully and you will see that the artist has used texture skilfully and imaginatively – and with obvious enjoyment. In some places the paint layer is so thin that the texture of the canvas shows through, the white ground imparting an extra brilliance to the glazed and scumbled paint. In others, the paint is much thicker and retains the special character of the brush, knife or finger with which it was applied. In places the artist has scratched back into the paint – to draw the delicate tracery of the veins in the rose leaves, for example. You must be prepared to improvise, to invent a technique to describe what you see. The tiny, bright-white florets of the spray

▷ The complex forms of stems, leaves and flowers are now convincingly established, the solid forms paraphrased and summarized in three or four colours. In some areas the artist has painted the negative shapes – the spaces between objects – and in others the positive forms. While dealing with the detail, he has also been concerned that each part of the painting should occupy its correct position in space. Sharp contrasts of tone and colour and crisp edges bring areas forward, while closer tones and less strident, more blurred colours settle back. It is important to consider the volumes and spatial arrangements even within a small mass like this bunch of flowers.

of cotoneaster presented a problem. If they were painted dot by dot with a small brush they would look too neat and regular, so the artist squelched on white paint with the tip of a palette knife, barely touching the canvas. Seen from close-to, the result is a very irregular and uneven application of paint, but from a distance it convinces without being distracting.

Finishing the painting

All the time the artist was concentrating on certain parts of the painting, he was aware of how those parts fitted into the whole composition. It is

△ The artist continues to develop the details such as the pot and the foliage while keeping the whole paint surface going. The crisp veins on the rose leaves have been softened so that they settle into the mass of foliage. The leaves and flowers seen against the white cloth have been worked up and have become an important element in the composition.

▽ White is important in this painting – the cool white slab of cloth in the foreground balances the band of red in the background. White is not just white: the cloth is a cool white, reflecting into the foliage and cooling the shadows; the white of the rose, on the other hand, is warm and creamy; while the cotoneaster is a brilliant white, almost matching the cloth. The white of the cloth is added last to prevent it becoming muddied – the white of the canvas was sufficient to achieve colour balances and arrangements. Thick white paint is applied with brush and fingers, cutting back around the leaves and flowers to create a crisp silhouette.

important to keep the whole painting going, and to remember that each piece of paint will affect and be affected by other pieces of paint. Put colour down and let it relate to what is there, but be prepared to come back and refine it. If you study the final painting carefully, you'll see that certain passages have been 'knocked back' because they attracted too much attention – the veins sgraffitoed into the leaves, for example, have been softened.

Check that the planes of your painting are well established, so that the foreground and background are integrated on the picture surface yet create the illusion of perspective. And don't forget the underlying compositional themes. The diagonals and angles discussed earlier provide an architectural framework that gives the composition solidity.

Another theme that emerged was the importance of the silhouette. Here the eye travels along the jagged and angular line which describes the top of the piece, but the bottom silhouette seen against the white of the tablecloth is equally interesting. The artist edited out the shadows on the right side to emphasize the counterpoint of the pattern of leaves and flowers seen against the white cloth. These are the sort of decisions you as the artist will have to make in order to produce a painting which is special.

△ *The artist spent some time considering the painting and then decided he liked the pattern of the flowers silhouetted against the white cloth on the right. He used thick white paint for the cloth and worked it around the leaves, flowers and stems on the right, giving them more impact by editing out the shadows. Flowers are an attractive subject, but you have to guard against producing simply 'a pretty picture'. By combining a rigorous approach to composition, with striking colour and an appealing paint surface, the artist here has created a painting of strength, vigour and imagination.*

PROJECTS

PAINTING OUT OF DOORS

Painting out of doors in front of the subject is very different from painting in the studio. There can be a variety of problems: the weather is unpredictable, and the light inevitably changes as the day progresses or as clouds come and go. Nevertheless, there is no substitute for recording your experiences immediately and, if you are interested in landscape as a subject, you will find this is something you will have to do from time to time. Painting from nature is wonderfully enjoyable and stimulating, and will provide you with an unlimited fund of material which can be developed further in the studio.

The English landscape painter John Constable (1776–1837) painted one or two pictures entirely in the open air, but generally oils weren't used out of doors because the whole process was so cumbersome. Until the beginning of the nineteenth century artists ground their own pigments or bought them from artists' colourmen in skin bladders. When the artist wanted to use the paint, he punctured the bladder and plugged the hole with a tack or bone afterwards. Bladders were cumbersome and inclined to burst – which is why women favoured watercolour, which didn't explode all over their clothes.

Mr Rand and the collapsible tube

The first collapsible tube was devised (*c.* 1841) by an American portrait painter called John G. Rand. The soft metal tube prevented the paint drying out, but best of all it was portable – a great boon to artists, who could now pack their oil equipment and paint out of doors with no difficulty.

The Impressionists and painting *plein air*

At the end of the nineteenth century the French Impressionists were consumed with a desire for naturalism. They sought to achieve this by analysing tone and colour and recording the effects of light on surfaces very precisely. They subscribed to various theories of light and colour, but most of all they painted *'plein air'* to record their 'impressions' of the natural landscape as accurately as possible.

Painting *alla prima*

The Impressionists rejected the traditional style of painting with carefully controlled layers over a monochrome underpainting, blended brushstrokes and a highly finished paint surface. Instead they applied patches of bright, high-key colour which blended in the eye.

Alla prima describes a technique in which the painting is completed in one session with opaque paint which does not allow an underpainting or drawing to show through or modify the top layer. It is a direct method, and each patch of colour is laid down more less as it will appear in the final painting. The paint is applied wet-into-wet (see page 56); some of the colours are mixed on the palette, but they are also blended or partly blended on the canvas.

One of the problems of working out of doors is deciding what to paint. In this busy boatyard there was plenty going on, and everywhere you looked there was something to entertain the eye. The artist started by making a series of charcoal and then charcoal and pastel drawings in a small sketchbook to explore the possibilities.

▷ *The strong compositional lines and good tonal contrasts of this subject attracted the artist's attention. The boat loomed above us in a rather dramatic way, its delapidated condition lending it a certain romantic appeal.*

The technique is fast, which means it is well suited to working out of doors. This is why it appealed to the Impressionists, anxious to capture fleeting changes of light and colour. They also delighted in the spontaneity of the process, and the way this was reflected in the freshness and energy of the paint surface.

The problems of working outside

There are many practical problems to overcome when you are working out of doors – the wind, the rain, the damp, the heat – and these should not be underestimated. You need to be comfortable if you are going to work outside for some time; you can't sit and do a two-hour painting in the freezing cold with your hands going numb, nor can you paint with gloves on. In those conditions you will have to paint in short bursts, allowing yourself regular breaks to warm up.

If you frequently paint out of doors, you will gradually collect all the equipment that is necessary: a lightweight easel, a folding stool and a bag containing all the things you need for your work. Don't forget to take something to eat and drink, because an empty stomach can be very distracting. In winter you'll need a flask containing a hot drink; in summer lots of fluids and a sun hat at least.

A car is useful, especially in uncertain weather. Not only does it allow you do carry much more kit; it also provides a haven from wind and rain – a sort of mobile studio.

Having found a location, you need to make the most of your time. Start by doing a brief analysis in your sketchbook. Look around to find the most interesting view, and remember, it may not be the prettiest. A spectacular view may not make a good picture – possibly because everything is too far away or there is no interest in the foreground. Don't forget that you can select and exclude; you

△ *We didn't have a prepared canvas of the right size, so the artist used the top half of a 30 in × 20 in (72 cm × 51 cm) canvas, giving us a painting which is 20 in × 15 in (51 cm × 38 cm). If you are short of time, it is sensible to work on a smaller scale, and if you are working away from home, small canvases are easier. to carry. He started by putting in the hull of the boat in reds mixed on the palette, the brushstrokes following the direction of the planking.*

don't have to put in all those pylons unless they add something to the picture! What you leave out is as important to your painting as what you include.

It can be very difficult to isolate the subject of your picture in a panoramic landscape. Where do you start? A viewfinder is a useful tool. By looking at the landscape through a frame, you can see which sections are potentially interesting. If you haven't got a viewfinder, make a frame of the thumb and forefinger of both hands and peer through that.

△ *The sky was constantly changing. For a few seconds the sunlight on the clouds created this strange effect which caught the artist's attention. He recorded it, and would decide at a later stage whether to retain it or not.*

▽ *The broad forms are established very quickly with fresh, juicy paint. The artist wants to get as much as possible down quickly and to cover the canvas.*

▷ *In this detail you can see just how descriptive the brushstrokes can be. They follow the forms of the hull and the propeller, and capture a sense of the speed with which the artist is working.*

Starting to paint

The idea of this exercise is to get a painting down as quickly as possible to make an accurate record of the scene and your response to it. Start with a toned canvas, using a neutral mid-grey tone or raw sienna. This should be prepared at home and allowed to dry. Acrylic paint is ideal as it dries within an hour.

An *alla prima* painting is painted working wet-into-wet and is completed in one go. Get as much as you can down as quickly as possibly, and don't concentrate on one part of the painting, but let your eye dance about the entire picture surface and out to the edges – work to all four corners of the painting and keep the whole thing going. You'll find that bits of colour from one part of the painting are picked up on the brush and travel over to another part of the painting. Don't worry about these accidental bits of colour; they will hold the painting together and actually imitate the way light bounces about in nature, reflecting colours from one surface to another.

Simplify and generalize as much as you can. Let a mass of green stand for a clump of trees and a band of another green for fields. By using a richer, lusher *mélange* of texture and colour in the foreground, you create the visual illusion that it is nearer to the viewer and thus imply a sense of space in the painting. Once you have completed this simple painting, you may decide to elaborate it, but quite often you will find that what you have down already is quite sufficient.

You don't always have to travel far from home to find a landscape subject for an on-the-spot *alla prima* painting. Your garden, a local park or even the view from a window will provide you with plenty of material. And don't paint it once and think, 'Well, I've done that, what next?' Paint it again and again. It will change with the weather, the season, the time of day, the way you feel, even the size of canvas or brush you use. You can often learn more by painting the same subject over again than by painting different subjects all the time.

Preparatory sketches

I asked Stan Smith to do a painting of the boatyard in which his studio is located. The weather was inclement and time was limited, so he had to work directly. He started by making a series of quick charcoal sketches to investigate the possibilities, and decided to make a rather dramatic painting by cropping in to a single boat.

△ *Artists are often thought of as rather otherworldly people, but in fact most of them are immensely practical. Without a sketching easel to hand, Stan propped his canvas on a discarded shopping trolley.*

△ *These touches of local colour add zest to the painting. Again you can see the way the strokes of colour are used to build up the forms in a very concrete way. The paint is wet and slippery and some of the brushmarks skid across the surface.*

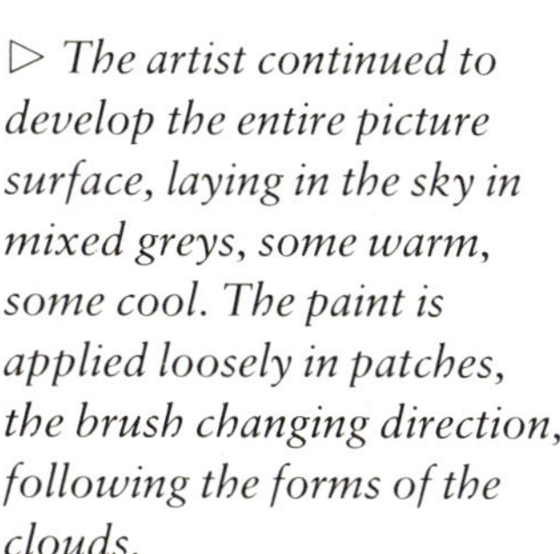

▷ *The artist continued to develop the entire picture surface, laying in the sky in mixed greys, some warm, some cool. The paint is applied loosely in patches, the brush changing direction, following the forms of the clouds.*

The boatyard

The weather on the chosen June day was unseasonal to say the least – bright, sunny spells interspersed by slashing rain and hailstones which thundered on the studio roof. Stan was phlegmatic about these adverse conditions, dashing out to paint when the sun was shining and working on something else in the studio when driven indoors.

In the limited time available a direct approach was the best, in fact the only, solution, so he worked on to a toned canvas with no underpainting. Using a brush and creamy paint mixed with only a little turpentine, he established the broad forms of the boat, the sky and the background. He worked quickly, progressing the whole painting at the same time. It is very important to keep the whole painting moving. If you pay too much attention to one part of the picture, it will become too detailed, and this will distract the viewer's attention and unbalance the composition. It will also waste time.

The secret of good *alla prima* painting is to keep the paint as fresh as possible. Study the subject carefully, mix the colour on your palette and put it down. You can adjust colours, scrape them off or add more on top, but try not to move the colour around too much on the canvas or it will look tired and overworked and the colours will become sludgy. Look at the details of this picture carefully and you will see that though the overall colour is subtle, each dab of colour is clean and fresh and has been put down crisply and with conviction.

▽ Below the hull there are planks, barrels, stones and bits of discarded plastic. The artist develops this area of the picture, adding bright tones of cadmium yellow and cobalt blue, and raw umber and burnt umber for the darker tones.

△ With a fine brush – a rigger – the artist draws in linear details. The paint surface is still wet, so he applies the paint very lightly, drawing the brush across the surface.

Stan used a limited palette: light red, raw umber, oxide of chromium, cobalt blue, Prussian blue, alizarin crimson, cadmium red, yellow ochre, black and white. He found his colours by making careful judgements, comparing and contrasting one area of colour with another. Take the hull of the boat, for example. It is red. You might be tempted to put down a slab of red paint and work white and black into it to make some areas darker and others lighter. The result would be a dull paint surface and a very unconvincing image. Study the photograph of the boat. The prow is a very rich, warm red, the side is slightly paler and cooler, and the shadow underneath is bluey purple. Concentrate hard and put down exactly what you see, no matter how odd it seems. Squinting helps, especially in bright light. When you stand back to view the painting after a period of work, you will be pleasantly surprised. All those separate patches of colour which look meaningless when viewed from up close really do look like the hull of a boat.

△ *Compare this with the earlier picture and you'll see that the whole painting has been developed. The trees on the left are more detailed, the polythene-covered boat behind has been redrawn, the sky reworked, and the foreground and the area under the boat have been worked into.*

▽ *Again a section-by-section comparison of this picture with the previous stage will reveal the way the artist has continued to develop the whole painting. Some of the tonal contrasts in the sky have been softened, details of the boat have been made crisper and the brightly coloured canvases around the boat have been resolved, adding an important touch of accent colour. By adding details to the foreground around the propeller, the artist brings this area to the front of the picture plane, creating a sense of recession. The painting is wonderfully atmospheric, capturing the lowering sky, clear light and colour effects created by the peculiar weather conditions.*

INDEX